First Aid for Teacher Burnout

Offering clear strategies rooted in research and expert recommendations, *First Aid for Teacher Burnout* empowers teachers to prevent and recover from burnout while finding success at work. Each chapter explores a different common cause of teacher burnout and provides takeaway strategies and realistic tips. Chapter coverage includes fighting low morale, diminishing stress, streamlining grading, reducing workload, leveraging collaboration, avoiding monotony, using technology to your advantage, managing classroom behavior, advocating for support from your administration, securing the help of parents and community, and more. Full of reflection exercises, confessions from real teachers, and veteran teacher tips, this accessible book provides easy-to-implement steps for alleviating burnout problems so you can enjoy peace and success in your teaching.

Jenny Grant Rankin, Ph.D., teaches the PostDoc Masterclass at University of Cambridge and is a former junior high school teacher, recipient of "Teacher of the Year" award, technology coordinator, school administrator, and district administrator. She is also author of *Designing Data Reports That Work: A Guide for Creating Data Systems in Schools and Districts* and *How to Make Data Work: A Guide for Educational Leaders*.

Other Eye on Education Books
Available from Routledge
(www.routledge.com/eyeoneducation)

How to Make Data Work: A Guide for Educational Leaders
Jenny Grant Rankin

Designing Data Reports That Work: A Guide for Creating Data Systems in Schools and Districts
Jenny Grant Rankin

The 30 Goals Challenge for Teachers: Small Steps to Transform Your Teaching
Shelly Sanchez Terrell

Better Lesson Plans, Better Lessons: Practical Strategies for Planning from Standards
Ben Curran

101 Answers for New Teachers and Their Mentors: Effective Teaching Tips for Daily Classroom Use, 3rd Edition
Annette Breaux

Dealing with Difficult Parents, 2nd Edition
Todd Whitaker and Douglas J. Fiore

7 Ways to Transform the Lives of Wounded Students
Joe Hendershott

Mentoring Is a Verb: Strategies for Improving College and Career Readiness
Russ Olwell

What Connected Educators Do Differently
Todd Whitaker, Jeffrey Zoul, and Jimmy Casas

The Educator's Guide to Writing a Book: Practical Advice for Teachers and Leaders
Cathie E. West

What Schools Don't Teach: 20 Ways to Help Students Excel in School and Life
Brad Johnson, Julie Sessions

Get Organized! Time Management for School Leaders, 2nd Edition
Frank Buck

First Aid for Teacher Burnout

How You Can Find Peace and Success

Jenny Grant Rankin

Routledge
Taylor & Francis Group

NEW YORK AND LONDON

First published 2017
by Routledge
711 Third Avenue, New York, NY 10017

and by Routledge
2 Park Square, Milton Park, Abingdon, Oxon, OX14 4RN

Routledge is an imprint of the Taylor & Francis Group, an informa business

© 2017 Taylor & Francis

Library of Congress Cataloging-in-Publication Data
Names: Rankin, Jenny Grant, author.
Title: First aid for teacher burnout : helping current and aspiring teachers craving
    peace and success / by Jenny G. Rankin.
Description: New York : Routledge, [2017] | Includes bibliographical references.
Identifiers: LCCN 2016014839 | ISBN 9781138655461 (hardback) | ISBN
    9781138655478 (pbk.) | ISBN 9781315622477 (ebook)
Subjects: LCSH: Teachers—Job stress—Prevention. | Burn out (Psychology)—
    Prevention.
Classification: LCC LB2840.2 .R36 2017 | DDC 371.1001/9—dc23
LC record available at https://lccn.loc.gov/2016014839

ISBN: 978-1-138-65546-1 (hbk)
ISBN: 978-1-138-65547-8 (pbk)
ISBN: 978-1-315-62247-7 (ebk)

Typeset in Optima
by Apex CoVantage, LLC

This book is dedicated to the outstanding
K–12 teachers I had as a child:

Mr. Hal Akins,
Mr. Todd Huck,
Mrs. Joan Morrison, and
Mr. Charles Schiller.

Great teachers change lives;
thanks for changing mine.

Contents

Meet the Author

Award-winning educator Dr. Jenny Grant Rankin, who teaches the PostDoc Masterclass at University of Cambridge, has a Ph.D. in education featuring a specialization in school improvement leadership. She is an active member of Mensa and many educational organizations, and her career has focused on making teacher "pain points" (like data, assessment, and technology) less cumbersome for busy educators.

Dr. Rankin left a higher education career for a rewarding career in K–12 public education. She taught English at the junior high school level while also serving as the school's technology coordinator. She eventually became a teacher on special assignment, then a junior high school assistant principal, and then a district administrator for a 35,000-student school district in Southern California. Within each administrative role, Dr. Rankin took joy in helping teachers and administrators streamline processes and finding other ways to provide educators with support. Dr. Rankin then served as chief education and research officer (CERO) for Illuminate Education, an educational technology data systems company, where she was able to work with teachers and administrators at hundreds of school districts across the United States to make data and technology time-saving tools rather than added stresses.

Dr. Rankin's books, typically relating to improving tools to make educators' jobs easier, are listed at www.overthecounterdata.com/resources. Joining her books and book chapters, Dr. Rankin's papers and articles have appeared in such publications as ASCD's *Educational Leadership, CCNews: Newsletter of the California Council on Teacher Education (CCTE), EdCircuit, Ed-Fi Alliance Blog, EdSurge* (funded by *The Washington Post), EdTech Review, Edtech Women, Edukwest, eSchoolNews, GALA Journal: A Journal of the Gender in Literacy and Life Assembly, International Society for Technology in Education (ISTE®) EdTechHub, Mensa Bulletin Magazine, Mensa Oracle, OnCUE: Journal of Computer Using Educators (CUE), The Women in Literacy and Life Assembly (WILLA) of the National Council of Teachers of English (NCTE) Journal*, and conference proceedings.

Dr. Rankin delivered a TED Talk at TEDxTUM and presents annually at the U.S. Department of Education's Institute of Education Sciences (IES) National Center for Education Statistics (NCES) STATS-DC Conference. She has presented in five countries, including presentations at the American Educational Research Association (AERA) Annual Meeting; California Council on Teacher Education (CCTE) Conference; California Educational Research Association (CERA) Conferences; Carnegie Foundation Summit on Improvement in Education; Classroom 2.0's Learning 2.0 Conference; Connect: Canada's National Learning and Technology Conference; Global Learn Conference in Berlin, Germany; International Society for Technology in Education (ISTE®) Conference, K–12 Online Conference; Learning Revolution Conference; Leadership Innovation Event at Montfort College, Chang Mai, Thailand; Mensa Annual Gathering; National Council on Measurement in Education (NCME) Annual Meeting; OZeLIVE! Australia: Ed Tech Down Under Conference; Society for Information Technology and Teacher Education (SITE) Conference; Technology Information Center for Administrative Leadership (TICAL) School Leadership Summit; University of California, Irvine (UCI) Digital Learning Lab; University of California, Los Angeles (UCLA) and National Center for Research on Evaluation, Standards, and Student Testing (CRESST) Conference; Wonder Women Tech Conference; and others.

Winning Teacher of the Year was a favorite honor, as was having the U.S. flag flown over the United States capitol at the request of the Honorable Christopher Cox, U.S. Representative, in recognition of Dr. Rankin's dedication to her students.

Her recent awards include the #EduWin Award, EdTech's 2014 Must-Read Higher Education Technology Blogs List, finalist for *EdTech Digest*'s Trendsetter Award, SIGNL Award for Twitter Followers Momentum, and Association for the Advancement of Computing in Education (AACE) Academic Expert. Her research website is also included on MIT's concise List of EdTech Blogs and Sites.

Dr. Rankin has served as judge for the University of Pennsylvania Graduate School of Education's prestigious Milken-Penn Graduate School of Education Business Plan Competition and the California Student Media Festival (CSMF) sponsored by PBS SoCAL, Computer Using Educators (CUE), and Discovery Education. Dr. Rankin was also paid to examine alignment issues related to the Common Core State Standards (CCSS) summative assessments as part of the Smarter Balanced Assessment Consortium (SBAC) Alignment Study, and she also served on the SBAC Panel for Achievement Level Setting.

In addition, Dr. Rankin has served on research committees for the International Society for Technology in Education (ISTE), the Society for Information Technology and Teacher Education (SITE), and the California Council on Teacher Education (CCTE). She also serves on the Panel of Experts and the Advisory Board for the New Media Consortium (NMC) *Horizon Report*, honored with a special listing and acknowledgment in the reports. Dr. Rankin also served as reviewer for the *Handbook of Research on Innovations in Information Retrieval, Analysis, and Management* from IGI Global and is an expert reviewer (reviewing for the journal *Educational Researcher* and multiple awards) for AERA. She regularly shares new research at www.overthecounterdata.com and https://twitter.com/OTCData.

Preface

This book is for current and aspiring teachers who want to prevent or recover from teacher burnout while finding sustainable success at work. Fifty-five percent of U.S. teachers report their morale is low, and it is declining (National Union of Teachers, 2013), 40% to 50% of new teachers leave within their first 5 years on the job, attrition is increasing (Ingersoll, 2012), and half a million teachers leave the profession every year (Seidel, 2014). Additional statistics are featured in the upcoming chapter. Even Merriam-Webster Dictionary refers to teachers in its examples of how to use the word *burnout*. Teacher burnout is an international epidemic.

Surprisingly, there is no other, current book showing teachers exactly how to avoid or repair burnout in a way that acknowledges the demands of the profession. For example, books either focus solely on mindset (e.g., how to have a more positive attitude about demanding work), share stories without detailing specific strategies, and/or are not specific to teachers (e.g., covering burnout for multiple professions rather than just teachers).

Conversely, this book is *specific* to teachers and helps them with the *specific*, burnout-inducing issues they face in their specific jobs. For example, this book does help with mindset, but the majority of the book offers help with all of the external factors, too (e.g., easy steps to reduce workload—like exactly how to implement more efficient grading practices and time-saving technology—reducing stresses that lead to burnout). This book details specific, realistic strategies teachers can apply to alleviate any major burnout-inducing problem and find sustainable success at work.

The author leverages extensive research, experience (she was an award-winning teacher and has vast experience guiding teachers), successful teachers' stories and tips, reflection exercises, and even a bit of humor. The humor is not meant to make light of the serious subject of burnout but to give readers some levity in their already-taxing days. This book details specific, realistic strategies teachers can apply to alleviate burnout-inducing problems and find sustainable success at work.

Audience

This book is designed for two types of K–12 teachers in most countries:

- current teachers (most teachers experience some level of burnout, and the remaining teachers still need to prevent likely burnout from happening)
- aspiring teachers (who do not yet have their own classrooms but are currently learning about teaching and will want to prevent burnout)

Higher education teachers (who teach K–12 teachers) can use the book as a source of content for their curriculum and to assign to their students. School administrators and district administrators might also be interested as a means for better supporting their teachers.

Purpose and Uses

This book is intended to save teachers from burnout and help them find success at work in a sustainable way. The book can be read alone or within a higher education class, or it can be read as a school group (e.g., department), school, or district. The reflection exercises at the end of each chapter help make the book especially conducive to any of these formats.

Given its flexibility and accessible content, the book is also well suited for professional development formats. For example, the reflection exercises work well as discussion topics as participants connect their own struggles with recommended practices and the feedback of coparticipants. Readers can assess their growth via self-assessments (links provided in book).

Format

Chapter topics include mindset, classroom environment, overstimulation, grading practices, work volume, overcommitting, collaboration, monotony, having to find/create curriculum, technology, behavior (classroom management), issues with administration (site or district), and community and parent relations. These chapters are divided into topic areas relating to setting the stage, getting rid of the unnecessary, helpful tools and processes, and issues relating to other people.

The book's checklist-style presentation of specific strategies is designed to be applied directly to practice, and the reflection exercises at the end of each chapter help with this (while also working well for group discussions). Humor and inspirational quotes are used to enhance the book's appeal to already-busy teachers, and educators reading independently can selectively read chapters based on issues they face (as each chapter is devoted to a single issue).

The author leverages an assortment of special features to help readers connect with the content: for example, diagrams, callouts, tables, checklists, web links (e.g., for free resources, self-tests, etc.), confessions from different teachers to open/ anchor each chapter (each teacher's name has been changed to honor privacy, as has the principal who also shared her side), inspiring quotes, funny quotes, jokes, sidebars, and more. Ancillary resources are also available online.

References

Ingersoll, R. M. (2012, May 16). Beginning teacher induction: What the data tell us: Induction is an education reform whose time has come. *Education Week*. Retrieved from http://www.edweek.org/ew/articles/2012/05/16/kappan_ingersoll.h31.html?tkn=MTNF 24nJQybOEmGq0BEBYEdXQnGRz0lpZatl&print=1#

National Union of Teachers. (2013, January 2). *Teacher survey shows government going in wrong direction*. Retrieved from http://www.teachers.org.uk/node/17250

Seidel, A. (2014). The teacher dropout crisis. *NPR*. Retrieved from http://www.npr.org/blogs/ ed/2014/07/18/332343240/the-teacher-dropout-crisis?utm_campaign=storyshare&utm_ source=twitter.com&utm_medium=social

Acknowledgments

There is no job title within my career that I have been more proud of than that of teacher. So much of what I learned about teaching I owe to the colleagues who surrounded me as I served in this role. I thus extend my deep gratitude to the entire staff at Buena Park Junior High School. I could not have imagined a dearer group of people with whom to work. I witnessed additional miracle workers as I worked with teachers while in my administrative roles at Orangeview Junior High School, Saddleback Valley Unified School District, and Illuminate Education. I hope the teachers in those districts (and in those districts using Illuminate Education products) know their expertise inspired many of the recommendations in this book. I am grateful for the anonymous teachers and principal who shared confessions to open each chapter. Their honesty reminds us that even the best professionals struggle at times. I also give thanks to the veteran teachers who lent their wisdom to the book in the form of tips and strategies, such as the remarkable Marie Bammer, Jeanette Dreyer, Julie Duddridge, Christine Friedrich, and Lori Smock. I am also grateful to the teaching superstars who reviewed the book and offered their endorsements. I owe deep gratitude to the incomparable Dr. Gail Thompson and Rufus Thompson for their mentorship and kindness and to Dr. Margie Johnson for being a continual cheerleader and presenting partner extraordinaire. I thank Michael Walker, as always, for kindly providing my author photo. I also thank traveling teacher Lillie Marshall for her wonderful ideas and sources regarding teacher PR. These acknowledgments would not be complete without thanking my heroic husband Lane Rankin. Having won Teacher of the Year for the state of California, Lane has devoted his career to helping students from every professional role he has assumed. Though here I thank him for his role as husband, as well. As always, I must also thank my kids: Clyde, Zach, Tyler, and Piper Rankin. They are always enthusiastic concerning my endeavors, and they never seem to doubt my efforts. These efforts would be fruitless without the support of my mother, Nancy Grant. How I got so blessed as to have her as a mother, I'll never know. A big thank you goes to the Illuminate Education team for their encouragement and backing. I extend massive thanks to my incredible editor, Heather Jarrow, who makes me feel so blessed to call Routledge/Taylor and Francis home for my books. I hope all acknowledged here know how much I have appreciated their support.

eResources

 Keep an eye out for the eResources icon throughout this book, which indicates a resource is available online. Resources mentioned in this book can be downloaded, printed, used to copy/paste text, and/or manipulated to suit your individualized use. You can access these downloads by visiting the book product page on our website: www.routledge.com/proudcts/9781138655478. Then click on the tab that reads "eResources" and then select the file(s) you need. The file(s) will download directly to your computer.

Introduction

Help Is on the Way

Every time I flew with my young daughter, the flight attendant reminded me to put on my oxygen mask before my child's if an emergency hit. If we were to hit the water, the advice would be the same: I'd need to prevent myself from drowning before I could pull my daughter from the water. This advice is in the child's best interest, as my ability to remain functional and thus able to look after her is fundamental to her survival.

In my career as a teacher, I had more than 1,000 students, whom I regarded as if they were my own kids. There was no stewardess stopping by my classroom each day to say, "Take care of yourself first, or your students will lose you and all you have to offer them." Yet that advice is true for teachers. Over time, those experiencing burnout accomplish less and lose their ability to make contributions strong enough to deliver an impact (Schaufeli, Leiter, & Maslach, 2009). You need to take care of yourself for your sake but also for your students' sakes.

You Are Not Alone

Most teachers feel like giving up at some point in their careers (Rauhala, 2015). If you are an aspiring teacher, you are

Definition of Burnout

Merriam-Webster (2015, p. 1) defines *burnout* as:

- "the condition of someone who has become very physically and emotionally tired after doing a difficult job for a long time"

. . . and gives these examples of the term:

- "Teaching can be very stressful, and many teachers eventually suffer *burnout*."

- "the *burnout* rate among teachers"

Even the dictionary knows burnout most often applies to teachers.

Teacher Burnout Statistics

- Only 39% of U.S. teachers report they are very satisfied (the lowest in 25 years), and 48% of teachers report they are regularly under great stress (Metropolitan Life Insurance Company, 2013).

- A survey of more than 30,000 teachers by the American Federation of Teachers (2015) revealed 100% of teachers "agreed" or "strongly agreed" they were enthusiastic about the profession when they began their careers, yet only 53% agreed at the point in their careers when they took the survey, with those who "strongly agreed" dropping from 89% to just 15%. Also, 73% of teachers reported they are "often" under stress.

- Fifty-five percent of U.S. teachers report their morale is low or very low, and 69% of teachers report their morale has declined (National Union of Teachers, 2013).

- Teachers have too many things to do in a limited amount of time (Staff and Wire Services Report, 2013).

- The UK's Education Staff Health Survey indicated 91% of school teachers suffered from stress in the past 2 years and 74% experienced anxiety; 91% reported excessive workload as the major cause (a 13% increase from the last 6 years; Stanley, 2014).

- More than 41% of teachers leave the profession within 5 years of starting, and teacher attrition has risen by 41% over the last two decades (Ingersoll, Merrill, & Stuckey, 2014). This provides clarification to Ingersoll's (2012) famous estimate that 40% to 50% of new teachers leave within their first 5 years on the job.

- Fifteen percent of U.S. teachers (about half a million) leave the profession every year, and the rate is 50% higher (affecting 20% of teachers) at high-poverty schools than at schools in financially secure areas (Seidel, 2014).

- Losing early-career teachers costs the U.S. up to $2,200,000,000 every year (Haynes, 2014).

- Burnout is an international epidemic. An ongoing stream of research on teacher burnout comes from Africa, Asia, Australia, Canada, Europe, the

Middle East, New Zealand, South America, the U.S., and more. Researchers in each area note the problem's impact. For example, nearly half of teachers in India suffer from burnout (Shukla & Trivedi, 2008), and half of male and female teachers studied in southern Jordan suffer from emotional exhaustion associated with burnout (Alkhateeb, Kraishan, & Salah, 2015).

- A survey of more than 100,000 teachers revealed more U.S. teachers (nearly 66%) work with students who are at least 30% impoverished than in any other country; U.S. teachers also work with larger class sizes, for longer hours, and with less time allocated for planning and collaboration than teachers in other countries (Darling-Hammond, 2014).

- Teachers who do an excellent job are often working in unsustainable conditions (e.g., 60 hours per week, relentless stress, inadequate resources, lack of support or time, etc.; Herman, 2014).

- In challenging schools, teachers' job requirements and the intensity required to meet them are not realistic to sustain for more than 2 to 3 years (Riggs, 2013).

- TNTP (formerly The New Teacher Project) reported almost 66% of the nation's best teachers continue to leave the profession for careers elsewhere (Chartock & Wiener, 2014).

- Even when teachers are passionate, working in a very demanding environment leads to mental and physical fatigue that is hard to fight, affects one's attitude, and makes it hard to work with students all day (Neufeld-nov, 2014).

- Being an effective teacher likely constitutes the hardest job of all in our society (Glasser, 1992).

Q: How many teachers does it take to change a light bulb?
A: One, but only if the teacher doesn't burn out before the bulb.

wise to read this book to prevent getting burned out in the profession. If you are a current teacher who is overwhelmed, you are not alone. Consider the teacher burnout statistics listed here; teacher burnout is clearly a worldwide epidemic.

Many argue burnout is an unavoidable consequence of good teaching. For example, at "no excuses" schools where idealistic, energetic teachers work overtime to help struggling students, teachers typically leave after only a few years on the job (Neufeldnov, 2014). This book offers an alternative.

Help for Every Culprit

What causes teachers to burn out can vary, but there are common themes. Fortunately, there is much you can do to either prevent or recover from burnout, whether you are either:

- an aspiring teacher or
- a current teacher.

This book offers a chapter on each major area that could cause you distress on the job and gives you clear, practical steps to avoid or alleviate that stress. These strategies are based on research and on veteran teacher recommendations. When factors causing you to feel overwhelmed are outside of your control, such as longer work days, tools are provided to advocate for change.

Burnout Self-Assessment

If you are unsure whether you are experiencing burnout, take one of these free self-assessments:

- From Christina Maslach: http://www.mindtools.com/pages/article/new TCS_08.htm
- From Teaching Tolerance: http://www.tolerance.org/sites/default/files/general/Teaching%20Tolerance%2051%20ED%20Cafe.pdf

Whether you are currently in the classroom or working to get a teaching job, this book will help you conquer the areas of your profession that can cause you to feel overwhelmed. However, a merely neutral experience at work is less than you deserve as someone following the difficult path of teaching and thus changing precious lives. The purpose of this book is thus to do much more for you to help you:

- feel excited as you arrive at school each day.
- enjoy camaraderie with (and support from) your colleagues.
- know you are making a difference in the world as you watch your students thrive.

> "Inside a ring or out, ain't nothing wrong with going down. It's staying down that's wrong."
> — *Muhammad Ali*

The Northwest Evaluation Association (2014) found 90% of students believe their teachers care about their learning. The Bill and Melinda Gates Foundation (2014) found 85% of teachers said they became teachers because they wanted to make a difference in children's lives. You *can* make that difference without getting burned out in the process. Commit to following the strategies in this book, and enjoy the career experience that awaits you.

References

Alkhateeb, O., Kraishan, O. M., & Salah, R. O. (2015, May 27). Level of psychological burnout of a sample of secondary phase teachers in Ma'an Governorate and its relationship with some other variables. *International Education Studies, 8*(6), 56–68. doi: 10.5539/ies.v8n6p56

American Federation of Teachers. (2015). *Quality of worklife survey.* Retrieved from http://www.aft.org/sites/default/files/worklifesurveyresults2015.pdf

Bill and Melinda Gates Foundation. (2014). *Primary sources: America's teachers on teaching in an era of change: A project of Scholastic and the Bill and Melinda Gates Foundation* (3rd ed.). Retrieved from http://www.scholastic.com/primarysources/download-the-full-report.htm

Chartock, J., & Wiener, R. (2014, November 13). How to save teachers from burning out, dropping out and other hazards of experience. *The Hechinger Report.* Retrieved from http://hechingerreport.org/content/can-keep-great-teachers-engaged-effective-settle-careers_18026/

Darling-Hammond, L. (2014, June 30). To close the achievement gap, we need to close the teaching gap. *Huffington Post.* Retrieved from http://www.huffingtonpost.com/linda-darlinghammond/to-close-the-achievement_b_5542614.html

Glasser, W. (1992). The quality school. *Phi Delta Kappan, 73*(9), 690–694. Bloomington, IN: ProQuest Periodical 1761291.

Haynes, M. (2014, July). On the path to equity: Improving the effectiveness of beginning teachers. *Alliance for Excellence.* Retrieved from http://all4ed.org/reports-factsheets/path-to-equity/

Herman, E. (2014, July 25). Teachers can't be effective without professional working conditions. *Gatsby in LA.* Retrieved from https://gatsbyinla.wordpress.com/2014/07/25/lesson-4-teachers-cant-be-effective-without-professional-working-conditions/

Ingersoll, R. M. (2012, May 16). Beginning teacher induction: What the data tell us: Induction is an education reform whose time has come. *Education Week*. Retrieved from http://www.edweek.org/ew/articles/2012/05/16/kappan_ingersoll.h31.html?tkn=MTNF24nJQybOEmGq0BEBYEdXQnGRz0lpZatl&print=1#

Ingersoll, R. M., Merrill, L., & Stuckey, D. (2014). *Seven trends: The transformation of the teaching force, updated April 2014*. CPRE Report (#RR-80). Philadelphia: Consortium for Policy Research in Education, University of Pennsylvania.

Merriam-Webster. (2015). *Dictionary: Burnout*. Retrieved from http://www.merriam-webster.com/dictionary/burnout

Metropolitan Life Insurance Company. (2013). *MetLife survey of the American teacher: Challenges for school leadership*. New York, NY: Author and Peanuts Worldwide.

National Union of Teachers. (2013, January 2). *Teacher survey shows government going in wrong direction*. Retrieved from http://www.teachers.org.uk/node/17250

Neufeldnov, S. (2014, November 10). Can a teacher be too dedicated? *The Atlantic*. Retrieved from http://m.theatlantic.com/national/archive/2014/11/can-a-teacher-be-too-dedicated/382563/?single_page=true

Northwest Evaluation Association (NWEA). (2014). *Make assessment matter: Students and educators want tests that support learning*. Portland, OR: Author.

Rauhala, J. (2015, April 16). Don't quit: 5 strategies for recovering after your worst day teaching. *Edutopia*. Retrieved from http://www.edutopia.org/blog/strategies-recovering-worst-day-teaching-johanna-rauhala

Riggs, L. (2013, October 18). Why do teachers quit? And why do they stay? *The Atlantic*. Retrieved from http://www.theatlantic.com/education/archive/2013/10/why-do-teachers-quit/280699/

Schaufeli, W. B., Leiter, M. P., & Maslach, C. (2009). Burnout: 35 years of research and practice. *Career Development International, 14*(3), 204–220. doi: 10.1108/13620430910966406

Seidel, A. (2014). The teacher dropout crisis. *NPR*. Retrieved from http://www.npr.org/blogs/ed/2014/07/18/332343240/the-teacher-dropout-crisis?utm_campaign=storyshare&utm_source=twitter.com&utm_medium=social

Shukla, A., & Trivedi, T. (2008). Burnout in Indian teachers. *Asia Pacific Education Review, 9*(3), 320–334. Education Research Institute.

Stanley, J. (2014, October 13). How unsustainable workloads are destroying the quality of teaching. *Schools Week*. Retrieved from http://schoolsweek.co.uk/how-unsustainable-workloads-are-destroying-the-quality-of-teaching

PART

II

Setting the Stage

2

Mindset

"My Attitude Is (Only Partly) Everything"

Teacher Confession: "I used to eat lunch in the staff lounge, but not anymore. It's way too toxic in there. I need to vent like any teacher does, but no one in my school's lounge offers solutions to problems. I hear lots of 'it's because our student demographics are so bad,' 'these kids can't learn,' 'technology spoils the kids' brains so they can't focus,' and 'if their parents can't do their jobs at home, we can't do our jobs at school.' I'm not blind to the strains placed on my job by diverse needs, learning challenges, bad technology habits, poor attention spans, and bad parenting. And I get that my colleagues have plenty of reason to gripe. But I want to overcome the challenges, not just dwell on them."

— *Hera Nuff*

Teacher Confession: "The other day I heard myself say, 'I hate that kid.' He's just a kid, and here I was saying I hate him. I have never been so ashamed of myself. How had I become so cold? I want to care for all my students."

— *Dez B. Leaf*

In researching teacher burnout, I found a lot of commentary as opposed to evidence suggesting attitude is the main decider of whether a teacher gets burned out. This chapter will offer strategies for having a proactive mindset that will help as you implement each chapter's recommendations. However, I need to first be clear that a good attitude will not, alone, defy burnout.

Burnout is often caused primarily by the organization within which some-one works rather than by the individual (Skovholt & Trotter-Mathison, 2011). Asking you to "grin and bear it" while chaos and pressure reign around you

> "Don't waste a minute not being happy. If one window closes, run to the next window—or break down a door."
>
> — *Brooke Shields*

would not be humane or effective as a long-term strategy. Thus this book will help you actively troubleshoot problems around you that contribute to burnout. In other words, when reading this chapter, note:

- attitude is only part of the equation, and
- help is on the way for the rest of your circumstances.

Teachers have plenty of justifiable reasons to complain about their jobs. That is a fact that won't be argued in this book. Yet there are thousands of teachers who love their jobs. Loving your work as a teacher and experiencing peace and success on a daily basis are certainly within your reach. The first step is to ensure your mindset is primed for any changes that need to take place. Attitude might not be everything, but it certainly is a lot.

Avoid Toxic Traps

One of the primary hazards for burnout is the presence of negative colleagues, which can include negative superiors, and these stakeholders' cynicism and negativity can spread like an infectious disease (Skovholt & Trotter-Mathison, 2011). In this chapter's teacher confessions, Hera Nuff encountered such negativity in the staff lounge, whereas Dez B. Leaf battled a negative outlook within himself.

> "Do not allow people to dim your shine because they are blinded. Tell them to put on some sunglasses."
>
> — *Lady Gaga*

Some negativity culprits might even be your close friends. The following strategies can help teachers avoid toxic talk. Apply these strategies as appropriate for your circumstances:

- **Avoid complainers.** Trying to remain upbeat in the face of negativity is taxing and time consuming. Educator author Annette Breaux (2015) suggests claiming to be on your way elsewhere, such as to the bathroom, when a negative colleague tries to corner you.

A colleague might warrant avoidance or conversation shifting if he or she:

- regularly blames administration, parents, or students for issues within the classroom.
- seems to have "given up" on making this a worthwhile job.
- is an overall downer, usually seeing the negative in a situation rather than seeing (or searching for) the positive.
- cannot control his or her temper.
- spends more time complaining than focusing on solutions.

- **Avoid gathering areas where negative talk is commonplace.** For example, sometimes time in the teachers' lounge causes more harm than good. Since it is best not to isolate yourself, arrange for a regular lunch date in someone's classroom with a few teachers you regard as positive influences.

- **Suggest solutions.** When a colleague complains to you, first affirm the gripe (e.g., "That must be so frustrating; I've had that happen, too") and then model constructive thinking (e.g., "I find it helps to . . ." or "I wonder if it would help if you . . ." or "You might want to talk to . . ."). Each teacher makes a contribution to the school's culture, and you would be helping the culture, helping your own mindset, and possibly helping your colleagues find solutions.

- **Share your burnout efforts.** If a negative colleague is also a friend with whom you'd like to remain close, talk to him or her about your efforts to avoid burnout. Share what you've learned about the power of positive thinking and ask him or her to help you infuse positivity into your conversations.

- **Talk to your educator leaders if toxic conversation derails collaboration time.** For example, if staff meetings become gripe sessions, point out to your administrators that you find this discouraging. If grade-level or department meetings digress into toxic forums, tell your grade/department chair that you find this discouraging.

- **Identify your burnout triggers.** For example, if you feel especially exhausted after lunch, rethink the way you spend that time. If your sixth period is the most challenging, start applying this book's burnout first aid with that class period primarily in mind. If talking to your principal exacerbates you, forgo this book's recommendations to reach out to her until a later time. Triggers force us into a survival mode in which we are less effective, whereas identifying triggers can help us resist them (Schwartz, 2010).

Amend Toxic Thinking

Expansive research has shown that the view you choose to have has a profound impact on how you behave and the results you achieve (Dweck, 2007). For example, nurses who enlisted positive thinking and avoided negative thinking were found to prevent and alleviate burnout (Espeland, 2006). The same is true for teachers, who also work demanding jobs caring for others. One commonality among teachers who last in the profession despite its many obstacles is they remain hopeful about their role in society, communities, and students' lives (Nieto, 2015).

The following strategies can help you avoid toxic thinking. Apply these strategies as appropriate for your circumstances:

- **Decide things you cannot control are not worth thinking about.** For example, in this chapter's teacher confessions, Hera Nuff acknowledged the strains that students' at-home technology habits have on their attention spans. As a teacher, you cannot directly control how many hours of TV your students watch at home. Thinking about the problem is thus not worth your time or energy. Tweaking your lessons to be more engaging, or another project, would be a more worthwhile focus in this case.

- **Learn about growth mindset.** Read the research or books (e.g., Dweck, 2007) by Stanford University psychologist Carol Dweck. Having a growth mindset will help you better deal with challenges and help you excel. Not only do educators benefit from having a growth mindset but they model (such as through their comments and reactions) a growth mindset for their students. Students who have a growth mindset earn higher grades, show greater motivation in school, achieve greater academic success, and score higher on academic tests (Dweck, 2007).

Growth Mindset Definition

Growth mindset involves understanding that intelligence and abilities can be developed (as opposed to being "fixed" qualities) and has been repeatedly shown to lead to school success.

- **Find a healthy place to vent.** Professional venting can help you guard against burnout (Skovholt & Trotter-Mathison, 2011). Sharing struggles and frustrations with a friendly colleague can break a teacher's isolation and improve even the worst day of teaching (Rauhala, 2015). Share your frustrations with someone who will sympathize but who will also encourage you to overcome obstacles. In other words, venting about your job is not the same thing as wallowing in negativity or ignoring ways you can prompt change.

- **Journal your frustrations.** Skovholt and Trotter-Mathison (2011) found that releasing negative emotions through writing can help practitioners guard against burnout. Writing has an added benefit in that you can take a break after journaling, perhaps when you are too frustrated to think of solutions, and then revisit your words when you are feeling less angry and more open to solving problems.

- **Play the "swap it" game.** It's OK to have negative thoughts (you're only human!); you just don't want to get stuck there. When high school art teacher Christine Friedrich catches herself thinking about something negative, she stops herself and thinks about two positive things going on in her classroom instead. When you catch yourself stewing over a negative thought, try replacing it with a more constructive one (see, for example, Table 2.1).

  If thinking up a constructive alternative to each negative thought is too cumbersome, simply use Table 2.1's last thought ("Every obstacle can be overcome") or other mantra every time you catch your mind dwelling in a negative place. The more you repeat a mental exercise, the more likely it will occur automatically (Schwartz, 2010).

- **Find opportunities to laugh.** Infuse appropriate humor (the positive, nonsarcastic kind) into your teaching, or peek at a joke-a-day website (like the K–12 Teachers Alliance's www.teachhub.com/teacher-joke-day) between classes. Employing humor was found to prevent and alleviate burnout in the case of healthcare workers (Demir, Ulusoy, & Ulusoy, 2003; Puig et al., 2012).

> "To succeed in life, you need three things: a wishbone, a backbone, and a funnybone."
> — *Reba McEntire*

Table 2.1 Examples of Swapping Thoughts

Unconstructive Thought	Constructive Thought
My students just can't learn or grow.	Every student can learn and grow.
My students' parents don't care about them or their education.	Parents generally care very much about their children and want their children to succeed.
I can never be an effective teacher.	I can be an effective teacher.
My students (or I) face too many obstacles to succeed.	Every obstacle can be overcome.

Adopt Healthy Habits

There is a definite connection between how you treat your body and how you feel mentally. The following strategies can have a positive impact on your health and mindset. Apply these strategies as appropriate for your circumstances:

> "I'm so unfamiliar with the gym I call it James."
> — *Chi McBride*

- **Exercise.** Yes, exercise. Exercise:

  - improves executive function (e.g., being able to strategize, ignore distractions, manage and alternate between tasks; Guiney & Machado, 2013)

  - reduces anxiety in a long-lasting way (Smith, 2013)

  - provides relief from depression (and is in some cases as valuable as therapy or antidepressants; Cooney et al., 2013)

  - can actually reorganize the brain so it can better resist stress (Schoenfeld, Rada, Pieruzzini, Hsueh, & Gould, 2013).

  > "If you have a headache, do what it says on the aspirin bottle: Take two aspirin and keep away from children."
  > — *Roseanne Barr*

  Some teachers power walk as a group during their lunch break to recharge.

- **Establish healthy rituals.** Rituals work best when they are performed in a precise way and at a consistent time, and over time they will require less energy or conscious effort (Schwartz, 2010). Find rituals that help you deal with events that have occurred and/or prepare for events to come. For example, every morning when you first touch your classroom's doorknob, take a deep breath and remind yourself why you teach and that progress is more important than perfection.

  Countless studies recount the power of gratitude, so consider daily recalling ways in which you are blessed. If you are burned out, better days are surely ahead because you are taking positive steps to make it so.

- **Get enough sleep.** Sleep influences our effectiveness more than any other behavior, and adequate sleep makes people healthier and happier

  > "Be thankful for what you have—you'll end up having more."
  > — *Oprah Winfrey*

(Schwartz, 2010). Stick to a bedtime that will allow you 7 to 9 hours of sleep (depending on what best sustains you). If you typically take 1 hour to fall asleep, go to bed 1 hour earlier to account for it.

- **Wash your hands and get outside.** Physical debilitation makes burnout even harder to avoid. Kids are often less diligent than adults about keeping clean, and schools are swarming with germs. A University of Connecticut study involving 11 years of data revealed teachers have double the death rate from autoimmune disease often provoked by exposure to infectious disease, poor air quality, and old building materials like lead and asbestos than people in other professions (Delisio, 2015).

  Find opportunities like nutrition break and lunch break to spend time outdoors. If your classroom has windows, keep them open when it's warm. On nice days, take students out onto the lawn for group discussions. Develop a routine for hand washing (or at least use of hand sanitizer), and when you do get sick . . . *take that sick day.*

- **Replace emotional eating with healthy rewards.** Poor eating can make you feel sluggish and lower your self-esteem. Many teachers eat too much or make unhealthy food choices because they're seeking to nurture or treat themselves. When you give, give, and give some more in a job while not feeling as if you "get" much back, the urge to binge or eat junk food can be strong.

  Give yourself regular rewards with better consequences. For example, maybe at the end of the week you'll buy something you've been pining for, or maybe you'll start each day with home-brewed tea, or maybe you'll listen to a "guilty plea-sure" audiobook on your commute to work. Start your day with healthy protein (e.g., vegetarian based) for fuel to get through your day, and avoid sugar, which can cause your energy to crash. If diet is one of your biggest struggles, consider joining a program or pairing up with a coworker to get added support.

> "My therapist told me the way to achieve true inner peace is to finish what I start. So far I've finished two bags of M&Ms and a chocolate cake. I feel better already."
>
> — *Dave Barry*

Teachers I worked with once established a "Biggest Loser" contest to mirror the TV show by the same name. They had weekly weigh-ins privately with the colleague running the game, who would tell three of us (the game's "Prize Patrol") the weekly winner so we could surprise him or her in the classroom with a treat (e.g., we might cover the teacher's after-school supervisory shift the following week). The teacher who lost the most weight at the end of the school year won all the money his coparticipants had added to the pot ($25 each). The greatest win, however, was the staffwide focus on health and the support colleagues gave one another in this endeavor.

- **Play your own soundtrack.** Research suggests inspiring music can stimulate varied neurobiological systems to improve mood, motivate, enhance perception, and even create self-fulfilling prophecy (Bergland, 2012). Create a CD or playlist of songs that inspire you and listen to it regularly. Some suggestions from varied genres are provided in this book's eResources.

Reflection Exercises

The following items can be answered individually and/or discussed as a group. If you are an aspiring (as opposed to current) teacher, there is an eResource offering versions of this book's reflection exercises reworded just for you.

1. Reflect on which of your colleagues are overly negative. What strategies will you enlist to steer clear of (or influence) their negativity?

   _____

   _____

   _____

   _____

2. What are your burnout triggers? What ideas do you already have for tempering them? Return to this item after reading the rest of this book to add additional strategies you learn.

   _____

   _____

   _____

   _____

3. What toxic thoughts do you commonly have, and what are more positive thoughts with which you will try to replace them?

   _____ → _____

   _____ → _____

   _____ → _____

   _____ → _____

4. What healthy approach to venting will you enlist? Consider where you vent (e.g., to whom) and how you vent.

_____

_____

_____

_____

5. What unhealthy habits do you have, and what healthy habit or ritual will replace each of these?

_____ → _____

_____ → _____

_____ → _____

_____ → _____

References

Bergland, C. (2012, December 29). The neuroscience of music, mindset, and motivation: Simple ways you can use music to create changes in mindset and behavior. _Psychology Today_ and _the Athlete's Way_. Retrieved from https://www.psychologytoday.com/blog/the-athletes-way/201212/the-neuroscience-music-mindset-and-motivation

Breaux, A. (2015). Ten things master teachers do. _ASCD Express, 10_(23), 1–2. Retrieved from http://www.ascd.org/ascd-express/vol10/1023-breaux.aspx?utm_source=ascdexpress&utm_medium=email&utm_campaign=Express-11–08

Cooney, G. M., Dwan, K., Greig, C. A., Lawlor, D. A., Rimer, J., Waugh, F. R., McMurdo, M., & Mead, G. E. (2013). Exercise for depression. _Cochrane Database of Systematic Reviews, 2013_(9), 73–157. doi: 10.1002/14651858.CD004366

Delisio, E. R. (2015, March 23). Autoimmune diseases hit teachers hard. _Education World_. Retrieved from http://www.educationworld.com/a_issues/issues/issues227.shtml

Demir, A., Ulusoy, M., & Ulusoy, M. F. (2003). Investigation of factors influencing burnout levels in the professional and private lives of nurses. _International Journal of Nursing Studies, 40_(8), 807–827.

Dweck, C. (2007). _Mindset: The new psychology of success_. New York, NY: Ballantine Books.

Espeland, K. E. (2006). Overcoming burnout: How to revitalize your career. _The Journal of Continuing Education in Nursing, 37_(4), 178–184.

Guiney, H., & Machado, L. (2013). Benefits of regular aerobic exercise for executive functioning in healthy populations. _Psychonomic Bulletin & Review, 20_(1), 73–86. doi: 10.3758/s13423–012–0345–4

Nieto, S. (2015, March). Still teaching in spite of it all. *Educational Leadership, 72*(6), 54–59. Alexandria, VA: ASCD.

Puig, A., Baggs, A., Mixon, K., Park, Y. M., Kim, B. Y., & Lee, S. M. (2012). Relationship between job burnout and personal wellness in mental health professionals. *Journal of Employment Counseling, 49*, 98–109.

Rauhala, J. (2015, April 16). Don't quit: 5 strategies for recovering after your worst day teaching. *Edutopia*. Retrieved from http://www.edutopia.org/blog/strategies-recovering-worst-day-teaching-johanna-rauhala

Schoenfeld, T. J., Rada, P., Pieruzzini, P. R., Hsueh, B., & Gould, E. (2013, May 1). Physical exercise prevents stress-induced activation of granule neurons and enhances local inhibitory mechanisms in the dentate gyrus. *The Journal of Neuroscience, 33*(18), 7770–7777. doi: 10.1523/JNEUROSCI.5352–12.2013

Schwartz, T. (2010). *The way we're working isn't working: The four forgotten needs that energize.* New York, NY: Free Press.

Skovholt, T. M., & Trotter-Mathison, M. J. (2011). *The resilient practitioner: Burnout prevention and self-care strategies for counselors, therapists, teachers, and health professionals* (2nd ed.). New York, NY: Routledge, Taylor and Francis Group, LLC.

Smith, J. C. (2013, February). Effects of emotional exposure on state anxiety after acute exercise. *Medicine and Science in Sports and Exercise, 45*(2), 372–378. doi: 10.1249/MSS.0b013e31826d5ce5

3 Environment

"My Classroom Looks Like a Room Without Class"

Teacher Confession: "I like to say, 'there is a method to my madness' when people see my classroom, but the truth is that its content has gotten out of control. I move stacks of paper to make room for other stacks, and I can't always find what I'm looking for. I know I have to clean it, but the thought is overwhelming."

— *Kay Oss*

Teacher Confession: "I keep my classroom clean. There's nothing really offensive about it. But it just doesn't make me or the kids feel that 'at home' feeling."

— *Van Ella*

Kay Oss and Van Ella are just two examples of teachers whose rooms aren't carrying their weight. Consider whether your classroom fits any of the following descriptions:

- The room looks messy or cluttered.
- Posters/visuals are too juvenile or outdated.
- There's just something depressing about the space.
- I can't always find what I'm looking for, or it takes me too long to find items.
- I haven't changed the majority of what's on the walls in a long time.
- The arrangement doesn't suit some of the activities or processes I want to use with my students.
- The room doesn't promote my students' academic and behavioral growth.

If any of the above describes your classroom, it's time for a change.

Enriching your environment can lead to a 25% increase in brainpower (OWP/P Cannon Design & Mau, 2010). Benefits are experienced not just by you but by your students, too. A 3,766-student study in 153 UK classrooms revealed simple changes to classroom design accounted for 16% of a student's yearly progress (Barrett, Zhang, Davies, & Barrett, 2015).

Given the stress you face on the job, every resource that can make you feel better and make your job easier is worth tapping. Part of the solution lies in putting your room in order, which involves reflection on how the room can best suit your and your students' needs. You'll also want to develop systems that make the new look easy to maintain.

Make the Project Doable

A classroom overhaul takes time, on which teachers are short. The following strategies can help make the project more likely and manageable. Apply these strategies as appropriate for your circumstances:

> To achieve great things, two things are needed; a plan, and not quite enough time.
> — *Leonard Bernstein*

- **Steal time.** Start by finding something to take off your plate (e.g., maybe grading a particular assignment isn't vital) or shifting plans (e.g., maybe colleagues can lunch in your room rather than the usual location so you can all chat while you clean) so you aren't overly taxed by the time spent on cleanup.

- **Enlist help.** Helping hands cut your time and effort, so find some students interested in helping outside of class hours. Many students love the concept of decorating, and you can praise students for their efforts while they work. They'll feel good, you'll feel good, and (in a fresher classroom) your whole class will feel better.

  Custodial staff is often willing to help you lift or hang items, particularly if you're appreciative of their assistance. Though your teacher colleagues can also help, first try to get aid from those unlikely to also be experiencing burnout.

- **Don't forget to plan.** Planning well will save you time in the long run. Think of everything you'll need (e.g., ladder, measuring tape, pushpins, staple gun, tape, larger trash and recycling bins borrowed from the custodians, etc.) and arrange to have it all ready when you tackle your redecorating project.

Also spend time just staring at your room, imagining how different scenarios will play out (e.g., "If I move the homework scanner there, how will traffic flow as students walk in and then turn in their work?"). Then plan accordingly.

Prime Your Environment

"I like order. It allows me to have chaos in my head."
— Dwight Yoakam

If your environment is visibly chaotic, you are more likely to feel loss of control. And if overwhelming events occur throughout your day, you are likely to feel overwhelmed without positive points to offset them.

The following strategies can prime your surroundings for a calm and proactive mindset. Apply these strategies as appropriate for your circumstances:

- **Clean and purge.** Princeton University researchers found physical clutter in your workspace limits your ability to focus and process information and makes you less productive and more irritable (McMains & Kastner, 2011). As for students, removing clutter has been shown to improve test scores and increase on-task time (Morrison, 2015).

  Assess which items in your classroom are helping students most, and remove any that aren't carrying their weight. Give supplies and visuals you don't use anymore to newer teachers (that's how I got all of mine when I started teaching).

- **Freshen up.** Post new content on your bulletin boards, rearrange the desks, spritz some room freshener, add cheerful accents like plants or colorful pillows, come up with a cool decorating scheme, etc.

Teacher: "I seem to have misplaced my lesson plan amongst the papers on my desk."
Student: "What was the lesson about?"
Teacher: "About how you kids have to be more organized."

- **Have emergency lessons on hand.** Despite your best efforts, you might miss finishing a lesson on time (perhaps to sleep). To prevent stress and panic, keep meaningful lessons on hand that can compensate for an unfinished lesson component.

- **Let there be light.** The classroom's natural feel (e.g., natural light, aired out every hour, and

Password Tip

If you regularly type a password (such as to log into your computer daily), make the password an encouragement or reminder. This will embed the phrase within your routine. For example, these passwords would be appropriate daily reminders for some teachers' circumstances:

- ÷&Conquer
- =Time4me
- >obstacle
- <IMdoing
- +Mindset
- 1day@aTime
- 4getH8rs
- 6cess!
- ask4help
- cirQL8
- cre8peace
- D5lim8s
- deleg8
- ElimN8
- grati2d

- ignoreH8rs
- Iofthet!ger
- Ir0ck
- Iwillsur5
- justsAn0
- kRPDM
- never2L8
- noMtn2Hi *or* noValE2Lo
- progre7ergy
- serN!T
- skip1thing
- st8rue2self
- techENtra9
- U=OvrCmr
- UcanDo!t

These passwords contain at least one number or special character to increase security. Note that password requirements can differ in terms of accepted length and character types.

Answers: divide and conquer, equal time for me, greater than obstacle, less than I am doing, positive mindset *or* growth mindset, one day at a time, forget haters, success!, ask for help, circulate, create peace, defy limits, delegate, eliminate, gratitude, ignore haters, eye of the tiger, I rock, I will survive, just say no, *carpe diem*, never too late, no mountain too high *or* no valley too low, progressive energy, serenity, skip one thing, stay true to self, techie in training, you are an overcomer, you can do it a cool but comfortable temperature) accounted for most benefits to classroom design studied by Barrett, Zhang, Davies, and Barrett (2015), with a steady stream of natural light being the most powerful aspect. If you have butcher paper or posters covering windows for more display space or to limit student distractions, remove them. If you have blinds or curtains, resolve to keep them open.

- **Post words of encouragement.** Choose an encouraging quote or mantra (or series of mantras) and display it somewhere you'll see every day (such as on your bathroom mirror, above your laptop screen, or on your classroom wall). Consider turning your mantra into a password.

  Search for (e.g., Google) "growth mindset quotes" on the Internet, and you will find some highly encouraging mantras. If you don't feel appreciated, you might want to use a teacher appreciation quote from this book's eResources. A Huffington Post survey of 1,000 American adults revealed even 52% of the general public feels teachers are underappreciated (YouGov, 2015).

- **Leverage color.** Findings from multiple studies indicate specific colors can impact classroom activities; for example, calming yellow can assist learning, whereas blue can encourage collaboration (Morrison, 2015). See the color table and guide in this book's eResources to leverage color in your classroom.

- **Surround yourself with evidence of your impact.** In my classroom, I called the bulletin board beside my desk my "board of love" and covered it with drawings and sweet notes students had given me. Students loved seeing their gifts posted there, and it was a constant reminder (to all of us) of the loving relationship we shared. If you have a graph showing your class raised the most money for a district fundraiser or a photo of your students participating at the science fair, post it somewhere prominent. Savoring small victories in which you made a difference in students' lives has been shown to help guard against burnout (Skovholt & Trotter-Mathison, 2011).

Rearrange to Support Learning

Despite how vehemently some teachers insist their arrangements are the best, your classroom's floor plan is a very unique matter. Arranging your room in a format that works best for you can alleviate stress and make your job easier.

The following strategies can help you adopt a floor plan that will best support your and your students' needs. Apply these strategies as appropriate for your circumstances:

- **Facilitate cooperative learning.** Cooperative learning becomes a draining demand if your classroom doesn't make it easy. Traditional desk rows shout, "Expect this class to be boring, because this classroom is arranged like it's 1890." Use a room plan that allows you to more easily enhance instruction, like encouraging students to speak and interact. One of the best decisions I ever made as a teacher was to arrange my room in a huge "U" shape (see Figure 3.1, shown in color in eResources).

Students sat beside one another and could easily be grouped to work together and/or differentiate, and we used the middle of the room for learning "game playing" and more. I used this arrangement with the stickers and grouping strategies described next.

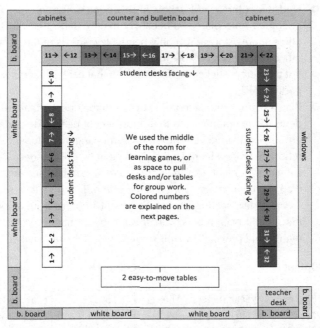

Figure 3.1 Example of Room Arrangement Indicating Which Stickers Are on Which Desks (Shown in Color in eResources)

- **Facilitate differentiated instruction.** Differentiating instruction can be an intimidating prospect for teachers. Fortunately, meeting students' different needs becomes much easier if your room plan makes it quick and easy to group students. Even better, you can use an easy sticker system to help. Read how easy the sticker system shown here makes it to group students appropriately and flexibly.

System With Ready-Made Stickers

Notice the colored numbers and arrows on my classroom's floor plan (Figure 3.1; color version in eResources). These represent the stickers I placed at the back of each desk's armrest. These labels work with almost any classroom arrangement (i.e., you don't have to place your desks in a "U" like mine). Just be sure each desk sticker clearly points to a partner desk.

There are just three steps to setup:

❶ Find the colored desk labels in this book's eResources. Have them color-copied onto plain, 10-per-sheet mailing labels (such as those sold in office supply stores). You only need a few sheets of labels, so your school office might even be able to give you some.

❷ Put a different sticker on each desk so that each sticker clearly points to a partner desk.

❸ Plan a seating chart according to one of the options that follows using students' demographics and their most recent performance data (e.g., place an English learner (EL) next to a same-language student who has been redesignated as Fluent English Proficient (R-FEP) for peer support, place a struggling student near the front where he can best see and get extra help, etc.). Changing from Option A to Option B, and vice versa, any time you create a new seating chart will prevent students from associating particular colors or numbers with specific performance. Using recent performance will prevent students from getting stuck or "tracked" in a category.

Option A

Stickers	Seat Students Who're
Even Numbers	Higher Performers (Paired Appropriately)
Odd Numbers	Struggling Students (Paired Appropriately)

Option B

Stickers	Seat Students Who're
Even Numbers	Struggling Students (Paired Appropriately)
Odd Numbers	Higher Performers (Paired Appropriately)

Any time you teach, you can now easily group students (for learning games, activities, homework distribution, stations, etc.) appropriately. Just use Table 3.1, which shows you ways to group students in whatever way best suits your particular task (i.e., use different rows for different activities, depending on your needs).

● **Example**: If I wanted kids to work at stations, where each of the eight stations contained four students with similar needs (and thus working on a station-specific project catered to those needs), I would group students according to the third-from-the-bottom row (on Table 3.1).

Table 3.1 is planned around 32 students, but the stickers allow for 40 students (and you could even make more), so you can adjust the chart to suit your class size. You might choose to use data on learning preferences, interests, and so forth, or to change students' seats for particular activities. Whatever your approach, having this sticker system in place will make student grouping easy when you need it.

Table 3.1 How to Group Students by Stickers Based on Needs

Needed Characteristics	Needed Grouping	Sticker Grouping	Examples of What to Tell Class
Students are **paired by mixed level** so one student offers **peer support** to the other.	16 Pairs of 2	Arrows (→ and ←)	"Turn to your partner based on where your arrow is pointing."
Groups are equally matched so it would be fair for one team to "compete" against the other or for each team to contain an equal mix of varied roles (e.g., each team has the same project, but has 1 leader, 1 recorder, etc.)	8 Teams of 4	Consecutive Numbers 1–4, etc. (color options also exist)	"Numbers between 1 and 4 are on one team, numbers between 5 and 8 are on another team,…"
	4 Teams of 8	Color (number options also exist)	"All pink are in one group, all green are in another group, all blue…"
	2 Teams of 16	Consecutive Numbers 1–16, etc. (color options also exist)	"Numbers between 1 and 16 are on one team; numbers between 17 and 32 are on the other team."

(Continued)

27

Table 3.1 (Continued)

Needed Characteristics	Needed Grouping	Sticker Grouping	Examples of What to Tell Class
	16 Pairs of 2	Every-Other Number	"Numbers 1 and 3 are together, 2 and 4 are together, 5 and 7 are..."
Each **group** contains students with **similar needs** and/or at approximately the same level so the same task, activity, assignment, station, or help can be given to all students in the same pair or group (e.g., 1 group is at a station where the task is a bit higher than grade-level, etc.)	8 Groups of 4	Color + Even/Odd Number	"All even numbers that are pink are in one group, all odd numbers that are pink are in another group..."
	4 Groups of 8	Color + Even/Odd Number 1–16, etc.	"All pink even numbers on this side of the room are in one group, all pink odd numbers on this side..."
	2 Groups of 16	Even/Odd Number	"All even numbers are in one group; all odd numbers are in the other group."

Q: What do a teacher and Mac-Gyver have in common?

A: Both can hang a poster, fix a laptop, and deliver a physics lesson with nothing but a thumbtack one kid threw and a wad of gum from under a desk.

• **Don't forget mobility.** No matter the arrangement you select, the desks are probably not anchored to the ground. You and students can move the desks for particular units or activities. Some desks are even designed for mobility, with wheels and the ability to snap onto other desks. Thus if a lesson is frustrating you and/ or the kids because of where the desks are, just move them.

- **If you're stuck with an arrangement that doesn't work, get one that does.** Talk to colleagues and administrators about what you have versus what you want. For example, a teacher with group tables might want to trade with a teacher who has single-student desks. Likewise, a teacher with a huge room might want to swap with a teacher whose room is too small for the desk arrangement he or she desires.

  School or district administration might be working on a grant for modern furnishings and tools, and you could get on their radar as a recipient (e.g., a test classroom). Also consider sources like www.Craigslist.com, colleagues, and friends for free or cheap couches, tables, lamps, and so forth . . . anything that will make your room feel special.

- **Consider funding.** If you're up for it, there are creative ways to fund special furniture and fixtures. For example, to acquire the innovative furnishings and technology in Laguna Beach's

  > "If bad decorating was a hanging offense, there'd be bodies hanging from every tree!"
  > — *Sylvester Stallone*

  classrooms, Michael Morrison (2015) leveraged varied sources, including donations from vendors looking for a test site to showcase their products.

Funding Resources

- Donors Choose (www.donorschoose.org) is a charitable site where any teacher can get funding for particular requests. More than 228,000 teachers have successfully raised funds for classroom projects on Donors Choose. Don't classify your request as "other," as those have the least chance of getting funded.

- Fund for Teachers (www.fundforteachers.org) can help you fund related professional learning experiences, like if you want to set up a blended classroom but don't know how to go about it. Since 2001, the fund has invested $22,000,000 to support 6,000 teachers in pursuing their self-designed learning fellowships.

Employ Systems

Well-thought-out systems help you keep your classroom clean while also helping you and your students to be more effective. The following strategies can help in this regard. Apply these strategies as appropriate for your circumstances:

- **Establish order.** Have a designated place for everything major, and label everything (even an index card taped in place and written on in marker can make a great label). Use containers to corral anticipated stacks or messes (many shoeboxes have the right dimensions to hold paper, don't cost money, and your students can decorate them during lunch). Arrange things so it's just as easy to put something in the right place as it is to leave it out.

- **Develop systems that make it easy for your room to stay clean.** Spend a lot of time thinking of the students' and your daily routines and what arrangement of containers and so on will work best to support those routines. For example, if students begin each class journaling, have each class period's journals labeled with student name on front and stacked in bins labeled by period and row, and ask the first students who arrive to put the journals on students' desks.

- **Train your students in simple, straightforward systems to keep things orderly.** For example, to exit our classroom, each of my students had to throw away a piece of trash on the way out the door (kids would scramble to pick up discarded papers, and they had a sense of ownership in our classroom's cleanliness). Those who didn't have trash would be let out, of course, but only after those who did have trash exited.

- **Consider going (at least partly) paperless.** If stacks of paper regularly amass around you, explore ways to reduce paper exchanged in your class. See the "Technology" chapter for tips on going paperless.

- **Don't wait until after class to straighten.** It's healthy for your students to see you caring for the classroom. As you circulate helping students, put things in their rightful places. This isn't the time for major cleaning, but if you tidy things throughout the day, you'll only have an occasional item to move.

Reflection Exercises

The following items can be answered individually and/or discussed as a group.

1. What items (e.g., visuals) in your classroom are best supporting student learning?

———————————————————————————————

———————————————————————————————

———————————————————————————————

———————————————————————————————

2. What about your classroom needs changing to be a more refreshing, effective space?

    _____

    _____

    _____

    _____

3. What room plan will you utilize that facilitates best practice (e.g., cooperative learning, differentiated instruction, nonlecture, etc.)? Draw it below.

4. What mantra or quote will you post for daily encouragement, and where will you post it?

    _____

    _____

    _____

    _____

5. What types of evidence of your impact will you display in your classroom?

_____

_____

_____

_____

6. Describe three systems you will employ to keep your classroom clean, orderly, and running smoothly.

A. _____

_____

_____

B. _____

_____

_____

C. _____

_____

_____

7. What beneficial items might be hard for you to get for your classroom? How will you acquire them, or are you able to easily get by without them?

_____

_____

_____

_____

References

ASCD. (2015, April). Tell me about . . . Good ways to communicate with teachers. *Educational Leadership, 72*(7), 93–94. Alexandria, VA: ASCD.

Barrett, P., Zhang, Y., Davies, F., & Barrett, L. (2015, February). *Summary report of the HEAD Project: Clever classrooms (holistic evidence and design)*. Manchester: University of Salford. Retrieved from http://www.salford.ac.uk/news/well-designed-classrooms-can-boost-learning-progress-in-primary-school-pupils-by-up-to-16-in-a-single-year,-research-reveals

Education Evolving. (2014). *Teacher-powered schools: Generating lasting impact through common sense innovation*. Retrieved from http://www.teacherpowered.org/files/Teacher-Powered-Schools-Whitepaper.pdf

Herman, E. (2014, July 25). Teachers can't be effective without professional working conditions. *Gatsby in LA*. Retrieved from https://gatsbyinla.wordpress.com/2014/07/25/lesson-4-teachers-cant-be-effective-without-professional-working-conditions/

McMains, S., & Kastner, S. (2011, January 2). Interactions of top-down and bottom-up mechanisms in human visual cortex. *The Journal of Neuroscience, 31*(2), 587–597. doi: 10.1523/JNEUROSCI.3766–10.2011

Morrison, M. (2015, January 27). An invitation to inspiring learning spaces. *Tech & Learning*. Retrieved from http://www.techlearning.com/contests/0007/an-invitation-to-inspiring-learning-spaces/68985

Neufeldnov, S. (2014, November 10). Can a teacher be too dedicated? *The Atlantic*. Retrieved from http://m.theatlantic.com/national/archive/2014/11/can-a-teacher-be-too-dedicated/382563/?single_page=true

OWP/P Cannon Design & Mau, B. (2010). *The third teacher*. New York, NY: Abrams.

Riggs, L. (2013, October 18). Why do teachers quit? And why do they stay? *The Atlantic*. Retrieved from http://www.theatlantic.com/education/archive/2013/10/why-do-teachers-quit/280699/

Skovholt, T. M., & Trotter-Mathison, M. J. (2011). *The resilient practitioner: Burnout prevention and self-care strategies for counselors, therapists, teachers, and health professionals* (2nd ed.). New York, NY: Routledge, Taylor and Francis Group, LLC.

TNTP. (2015, August 4). *The mirage: Confronting the hard truth about our quest for teacher development*. Retrieved from http://tntp.org/publications/view/evaluation-and-development/the-mirage-confronting-the-truth-about-our-quest-for-teacher-development?utm_source=EdsurgeTeachers&utm_campaign=af0dda9d1b-Instruct+182&utm_medium=email&utm_term=0_3d103d3ffb-af0dda9d1b-292335873

YouGov. (2015). *Poll results: Teachers*. Retrieved from https://today.yougov.com/news/2015/05/01/poll-results-teachers

Overstimulation

"My Brain Needs a Union Rep"

Teacher Confession: "I'm always 'on.' Students are waiting by my door when I get to school, and the whole day is an onslaught of kids and adults wanting things from me. By lunch, my inbox is so loaded I spend the whole hour responding to parents and coworkers, but more emails keep coming. My phone beeps and beeps at me as more messages from assorted apps come in. This continues when I'm at home, being further tugged at by my kids and wife. My mind has no rest. Even my sleep is restless."

— *Luke Adam Gogh*

The word "onslaught" Luke Adam Gogh uses aptly describes the way in which teachers' mental capacity is stretched to the limit by constant, diverse demands. This onslaught is compounded by technology, which increasingly carries the danger of overstimulation even as it helps us with conveniences.

Yet our brains need rest. Not prioritizing which information one affords his or her attention reduces cognitive capacity and effectiveness (Schwartz, 2010). Simply put, overstimulation is not fun. It fosters burnout and should be avoided through conscientious, targeted efforts.

Set Boundaries for Others

If you don't place restrictions on when and where others can enlist your help, you can end up serving everyone but yourself. The following strategies can help you set healthy boundaries that give you and your brain a rest. Apply these strategies as appropriate for your circumstances:

- **Seize lunchtime.** I used to spend the lunch break with my students, helping them with homework and hanging out. It was great for them (and I enjoyed the time, too), but the long-term effects on my workload and stress were significant. When I took lunchtime back for myself, I could

> "Try putting your iPhones down once in a while, and look in people's faces. People's faces will tell you amazing things."
> — Amy Poehler

make those 5-minute copies weighing on my mind. I could have a laugh with colleagues and share the day's challenges, making troubles easier to bear.

Special education teacher Lori Smock says taking a mental break to eat lunch while connecting with colleagues, bouncing around ideas, and getting input, is the number-one way she combats burnout. Elementary teacher Jeanette Dreyer, who tries not to work through recess and lunch, describes it as "very important" that she leaves the room to have lunch with colleagues.

Teachers are given very little time for themselves, so they need to truly take all that is given. Find a time other than lunch for students to reach you, such as during your morning cafeteria line duty. If that isn't possible, promise to be in your classroom 5 minutes before lunchtime's ending bell rings. You can then answer quick questions and refer students to whatever sources are in place for added help (e.g., after-school tutoring).

- **Advocate for reduced email.** If all-school emails are a problem (e.g., teachers sending jokes or announcements to the whole staff when not all staff necessarily want the emails), ask your administrators to enforce a policy of acquiring administrators' consent before sending all-staff emails.

Some districts make all-staff email shortcuts (e.g., when you email "AllTeachers@ . . . " the email goes to all teachers) only available to administrators so they're less likely to be overused. This is something you can suggest if such an email shortcut is being used by everyone.

If administrators aren't able to help you, you can create email filters to reduce distractions. For example, emails on which you are only CC'd can skip your inbox to be automatically archived.

Set Boundaries for Yourself

Setting boundaries for yourself can be much harder than setting them for others. After all, who but you will know if you violate those boundaries? Thus these

> "You cannot be really first rate at your work if your work is all you are."
>
> — *Anna Quindlen*

strategies require special diligence. It can help to tell others (such as a spouse or your kids) about your boundaries or even to set them together.

The following strategies can help you set healthy personal boundaries to give your brain a break. Apply these strategies as appropriate for your circumstances:

- **Put down the device.** Remember when you were young, and you survived without a technological device permanently attached to your palm? Allowing ourselves to be constantly at the beck and call of beeps, buzzes, and alerts from our phones, tablets, or other gadgets is mentally unhealthy. Your brain needs time to think, to wander, to ponder, and to just rest.

Determine which devices have enslaved you and set firm limits on how you use them. For my husband and me, this was our phones. Thus when my husband and I get home in the evening, we instantly put our phones in the kitchen drawer. This way it doesn't take much willpower to resist checking our phones, and we can still hear them ring in the event of an emergency. Put your especially tempting devices in a drawer during family time, and leave them there during most evenings.

- **Limit social media.** Social media like Facebook, Twitter, Pinterest, Instagram, Snapchat, and the like can be useful tools and are even promoted in this book. However, just like food, they can be vices if used in excess.

No matter the device you use to access it, social media can be a time hog. You and your brain need extended periods during which you are free to reflect, ponder, and daydream. Such moments of peace help you problem solve and are essential to mental health.

As much as you might enjoy and even benefit from your social media drug of choice, place restrictions on your use. If you overuse social media, consider these tips:

- Commit to a pattern in which you set aside the device you use to access social media.
- Remove the app or link (through which you access it) from one of your devices, such as from your phone, tablet, or computer so that it remains the one device from which you don't check the account.
- Reevaluate the social media you use and consider if one account is worth dropping. For example, if you get a lot of PD and enjoyment from Twitter

but find an online forum more time consuming and less valuable, drop the forum.

- **Don't tote the work home.** Leave your work at school. I find this to be one of the hardest suggestions in this book to follow. If your school schedule doesn't give you a planning period or hour, this is especially difficult. Four tips can help in either case:

  - Only take work home when it 100% has to (and thus will) be done there. I took work (e.g., homework, lesson planning, etc.) home countless times when it just sat in my car or by the door and never got touched. You don't need a physical reminder of your workload haunting you at home. Leave work at school unless there is no way you won't tackle it at home. Meanwhile, pay special attention to this book's "Grading" and "Volume" chapters for strategies that stop your work from accumulating.

  - If you must take work home, only take home a portion of it. Cameron (2014) suggests setting realistic grading goals, such as only taking home 10 to 15 papers a night if you know that's your grading limit rather than bringing home the whole stack of 50, which otherwise contributes to exhaustion.

  - Use school hours for the least-fun stuff, and take the most-fun stuff home. For example, I hated grading but loved lesson planning. Getting my grading over with at school and then lesson planning at home with music playing and my dogs lying at my feet made home time a little more sacred.

  - This book recommends using lunchtime to decompress with colleagues. That is an important guideline to follow, but allow yourself to break it when you fall especially far behind. It is better to miss lunch with colleagues than it is to miss quality time with your family after hours. Consider occasional compromises like grading papers during lunch in your colleagues' company while they do the same.

- **Limit when and where work email can reach you.** Email is one of the most common sources of work-related interruption, and we must consciously put limits on when we will allow it to distract us (Schwartz, 2010). For example, check your email at designated times per day and none others (and most of all, resist the urge to peek at them during class).

Sociologist Christine Carter suggests scheduling 20-minute blocks of time no more than five times per day to check and respond to email, particularly before beginning a project so you aren't tempted to break concentration (Oumanski, 2015). Renowned teacher Vicki Davis (2014) suggests fending off burnout by checking email twice per day and not syncing school email with your smartphone. This last suggestion can be especially powerful in improving the quality of your nonwork time so you have time to rest and recharge. The same suggestion can be applied to your tablet (e.g., iPad) or other device through which work email might otherwise pester you.

Place limits on your email use away from work, such as not checking email after hours or on the weekend. Share this arrangement with your family and/or partner to help you stick to it.

- **Deliberately focus on one thing at a time whenever possible.** Teachers are constantly torn in multiple directions, particularly during time with students ("Teacher, I need help," "Teacher, I need another homework copy," "Teacher, why are you pouring aspirin into your mouth?"). Mindfulness expert Dr. Kristen Race notes multitasking takes a toll on our brains, which must go back three or four steps to reorganize each time we change tasks, which is stressful and inefficient (Oumanski, 2015). Whenever possible, such as when you are working alone, select one task to work on and tell yourself you won't swap to a new task until you're done. You might get interrupted nonetheless, but you can avoid the interruptions within your control (like jumping to the grading pile looming before you or taking "just a peak" at email). It can help to turn off email notifications (that beep on your laptop as new emails arrive) and keep your desk clear of pending tasks.

- **Choose an instructional style that works with your personality.** Whatever your personality and preferences, there is a successful teaching style that will work for both you and students. For example, introverted teachers might abhor a classroom where students are constantly working as groups, making messes in maker spaces, or other chaotic teaching approaches (just as not every student prospers in those environments). In fact, introverted teachers experience higher levels of burnout and emotional exhaustion (Cano-Garcia, Padilla-Muñoz, & Carrasco-Ortiz, 2004), which many attribute to the shift away from lecture formats known to stifle most students. These teachers' solution can be to allow students to opt to collaborate but to do so in soft-speaking groups just as they would converse in a library. Whatever your personality, there is a way you can teach that suits both you and your students.

- **Find a way to have a life.** Teachers are less likely to be able to deliver high-quality instruction if they do not decompress outside of work (Neufeldnov, 2014). When all of a teacher's waking hours are devoted to work, the teacher is primed for burnout; teachers should instead skip work on the weekends and maintain their personal roles and joys (Rauhala, 2015). Elementary teacher

Jeanette Dreyer fends off burnout by balancing her life with nonschool relationships and activities, such as her faith community and personal hobbies.

You might tense up when you read this strategy and think, "I have too many work demands to find time for myself away from work." If that is the case, pay special attention to the "Goodbye, Fluff" chapters in this book. Those chapters will offer you the most help in cutting down your work demands, and other chapters will offer additional support.

> "I don't believe in email. I'm an old-fashioned girl. I prefer calling and hanging up."
> — Sarah Jessica Parker as Carrie Bradshaw

Also establish limits for any work you do at home. English teacher Lisa Chesser (2014) suggests teachers might set the boundary of not planning lessons, grading, or reading emails during a 3-hour window while at home.

Be sure you don't shortchange yourself and settle for less personal time than you need. Continue to perfect your efficiency and cut demands whenever you have the power to do so. You need time for family, friends, and yourself.

Employ Systems

When thoughts, worries, or "to do" items weigh on your mind, it is hard to relax and rejuvenate. Set up systems to record thoughts and funnel them into appropriate places, to address later, so your mind can be free of them in the meantime.

The following strategies can help you set up systems that will unburden your brain. Apply these strategies as appropriate for your circumstances:

- **Keep a to-do list.** It is hard to find mental rest when obligations are on your mind, particularly when you worry about forgetting them. Maintaining a to-do list helps free your mind of such worries, and helps ensure important tasks don't slip through the cracks.

Schwartz (2010) notes agenda setting can help us prioritize information worthy of our attention and sidestep burnout effects. In fact, renowned teacher Vicki Davis (2014) lists making a schedule and priority list as one of the top 12 ways to fend off

> "I love deadlines. I like the whooshing sound they make as they fly by."
> — Douglas Adams

burnout. Rauhala (2015) gives a prioritized list, on which you complete the top three tasks, as one of five ways to recover when you experience a bad day of teaching, noting the physical act of writing offers a sense of control.

To discourage burnout, your list should function as an assistant rather than a harassment. You don't want it to become one more thing to fan the flames of stress. To promote its positive role, keep your list's size small by including only essential items.

Though you might choose to begin with a traditional notepad, easy-to-use technology tools can help your list work better for you. For example, your list should be easy to access any time. The "notes" feature on your smartphone is ideal for lists because it is always with you, and a Google Doc (see the "Technology" chapter for details) is also ideal because it can be accessed through any device with Internet access. Technology also makes it easy to reprioritize (i.e., move) items on the list. If you are tech savvy, you might also choose to use a Google Doc spreadsheet with different columns/categories by which you can sort items.

Unlike social media, it is less stressful to be able to access your list (and cross items off) when you need to, so syncing with your devices is recommended. The same is true of calendars, discussed next.

● **Maintain a calendar.** Having a clear account of pending deadlines allows you to plan efficiently and avoid the stress of unwelcome surprises. A calendar is another way to keep pending items off your mind and stored in a place where they won't take you by surprise. Meetings with colleagues, school events, conversations with parents, standardized tests, and major deadlines are examples of the many events teachers can calendar to be prepared.

Again, technology can make a calendar work well for you. Use an online calendar that syncs with all your related devices and programs. For example, I can use my Google Calendar when I'm on my laptop and also when I accept an invitation through my Gmail (www.gmail.com) email account or while I'm on my smartphone.

Many school districts offer Microsoft Outlook (www.microsoft.com/en-us/outlook-com) for similar function. Using a calendar that's compatible with all your devices makes it easy to access and keep current. It also makes it easy to add appointments to your calendar. Describe your needs to your school's or district's tech support for recommendations on what calendars will work best for you and your devices.

● **Take advantage of email features.** Most email accounts allow you to set up filters that will automatically file or archive (similar to delete but still accessible) unwanted emails as they arrive. For example, if you have a software account that sends you daily product information you don't want, you can create a filter that forces these emails to automatically bypass your inbox entirely.

Reflection Exercises

The following items can be answered individually and/or discussed as a group.

1. Identify areas in which others infringe on your time when that time should be yours alone. Describe how you will set boundaries to make that time your own again.

   _____

   _____

   _____

   _____

2. Pick (✓) three distractions with which you are prone to struggle and explain how you will prevent them from stealing an excessive amount of your time.

   ● devices (smartphone, tablet, laptop, etc.)

   ● social media

   ● email

   ● work (toted home to work on there)

   ● work time (infringing on home time)

   ● other: _____

   _____

   _____

   _____

   _____

3. Describe how you will (or do) keep track of important pending tasks you need to complete. This method should be one that will prove most efficient for you, even if it requires advancing your technology skills and comfort level.

   _____

   _____

   _____

   _____

4. Describe how you will (or do) maintain a calendar of important upcoming events. This method should be one that will prove most efficient for you, even if it requires advancing your technology skills and comfort level.

_____

_____

_____

_____

5. In the email account you currently use for work, list the steps required to set up an inbox filter for unwanted emails. You might need to get help from someone or search online for directions.

A. _____

_____

_____

B. _____

_____

_____

C. _____

_____

_____

References

Cameron, K. (2014, November 14). 5 ways to take the grind out of grading papers. _Classroom 2.0_. Retrieved from http://www.classroom20.com/forum/topics/5-ways-to-take-the-grind-out-of-grading-papers-1

Cano-Garcia, F. J., Padilla-Muñoz, E. M., & Carrasco-Ortiz, M. A. (2004, September 11). Personality and contextual variables in teacher burnout. _Personality and Individual Differences, 38_, 929–940. doi: 10.1016/j.paid.2004.06.018

Chesser, L. (2014, March 18). 25 tricks to stop teacher burnout. _InformED_. Retrieved from http://www.opencolleges.edu.au/informed/features/25-tricks-to-stop-teacher-burnout/#ixzz31i2ITdLO

Davis, V. (2014, May 20). 12 choices to help you step back from burnout. _Edutopia_. Retrieved from http://www.edutopia.org/blog/12-choices-step-back-from-burnout-vicki-davis?utm_source=SilverpopMailing&utm_medium=email&utm_campaign=022515%20enews-A%20sm%20gm&utm_content=&utm_term=blog1&spMailingID=10733072&spUserID=MzgwNjgyODYwNjUS1&spJobID=481863955&spReportId=NDgxODYzOTU1S0

Neufeldnov, S. (2014, November 10). Can a teacher be too dedicated? *The Atlantic*. Retrieved from http://m.theatlantic.com/national/archive/2014/11/can-a-teacher-be-too-dedicated/382563/?single_page=true

Oumanski, P. (2015, June). 43 ways you're not really helping. *Real Simple, 16*(6), 142–149.

Rauhala, J. (2015, April 16). Don't quit: 5 strategies for recovering after your worst day teaching. *Edutopia*. Retrieved from http://www.edutopia.org/blog/strategies-recovering-worst-day-teaching-johanna-rauhala

Schwartz, T. (2010). *The way we're working isn't working: The four forgotten needs that energize*. New York, NY: Free Press.

PART

III

Goodbye, Fluff

Grading

"My Hobbies Are Grading, Grading, and More Grading"

Teacher Confession: "I teach math and I can't get to every student in the room, in every class period, on every day. I have to watch how each student solves each math problem. That's why my feedback on students' homework is pivotal—it's my way to 'be' there for each student. The problem is I'm overwhelmed by towering stacks of papers to grade. I'm always grading, yet I'm always behind on grading. I need weekends to barely keep up, and I'm crushed when students don't even read my comments."

— *Mark N. Sirs*

Teacher Confession: "It takes forever just to read my students' writing homework let alone make grammatical and spelling corrections, and then comment on style, composition, etc. There is just too much to do."

— *Alotta Marx*

According to the U.S. Department of Labor's Bureau of Labor Statistics (Krantz-Kent, 2008):

- Teachers are more likely than other professionals to continue their work at home on an average day (30% of teachers compared to 20% of other full-time professionals).
- Public school teachers spend 20% of their working time grading student work; this is surpassed only by classroom preparation (30% of time) and actual teaching in the classroom (25% of time).

Twenty percent of your time is a lot of time. According to a 100,000-teacher survey, U.S. teachers work an average of 45 hours per week (1 hour per day more than the global average of 38 hours per week; Darling-Hammond, 2014). This amounts to 9 hours per work day. That means you likely spend nearly 2 hours per day grading student work. If you could shave much of this time off your schedule, you would likely feel less overworked and less likely to burn out.

There are many who will argue that grading student work 2 or more hours per day is necessary. Those same people might argue against some of this book's suggestions for grading, arguing it serves students best to have a teacher's personalized feedback for every student on every assignment they ever complete. Yes, it would be ideal for every student to get highly personalized feedback from every teacher on every assignment. But unless every teacher is assigned to only one student, that expectation will strangle the teacher trying to meet it through conventional means. Better the teacher be refreshed, energized, and able to deliver a killer lesson that engages all students so they can apply the learned concept correctly from the start. Then, from that position, the teacher can begin to implement technologies and processes that make individualized feedback more efficient and realistic.

> **Student:** Teacher, you assign yourself too much homework.
> **Teacher:** What do you mean?
> **Student:** Well, this assignment takes each student only 20 minutes, but the stack takes you 5 hours to grade.

> **Q:** What's the difference between doing taxes and grading papers?
> **A:** You only have to do taxes once a year, and if the IRS disputes something, it doesn't call your principal.

Challenge Your View of Grading

It is likely hard to let go of your established grading practices. You selected them for a reason, right? In light of the need to avoid burnout, for which simplifying and reducing grading holds much potential, it is worth reevaluating your grading habits. To do this, it is helpful to first reconsider your views on grading and the worth you afford it.

The following strategies can help you lessen the role grading plays in your students' educations. Apply these strategies as appropriate for your circumstances:

- **Consider feedback turnaround time.** Calculate the exact amount of time that passes between the moment your students complete an assignment and the moment that graded assignment is back in their hands. Homework comments are usually so late, whereas it's best for a teacher to intervene with feedback at the moment kids are thinking.

I'm not arguing all homework is bad, but homework (particularly minimally effective homework) often plays too dominant a role in education. Critically evaluate each assignment's likelihood of truly enhancing student learning. You will likely identify many assignments you can skip or replace with projects more likely to ignite students' interest and learning.

● **Consider the likelihood of students reexamining each item and its answer.** When the impact assignments have on students' grades is their most emphasized quality, students tend to care most about the assignment's score when it is handed back to them. Particularly if numerous assignments are handed back to students at the same time, students rarely revisit returned assignments with the same intensity of thought they gave the assignments while completing them.

Even if you go back over questions and answers as a class, students are rarely as committed to understanding each question in the same way they first were (when how they answered would affect their grades). Also, going back over homework or tests as a class often represents a stale use of classroom time, during which time students are no more than marginally engaged.

"For elementary-school kids, there is really no correlation between homework and achievement . . . From middle school on up, we start to see a correlation . . . [but it] fades after 90 minutes for middle school and two hours for high school."
— *Denise Pope, Ph.D., Stanford Graduate School of Education* (Passarella, 2015, pp. 150–151)

● **Consider the likelihood of students' reading comments.** Most teachers have experienced the disappointment of writing thoughtful feedback on assignments only to find them in the trash immediately after class. Sometimes these comments are given a cursory glance, but often they aren't read at all.

Usually the students most in need of processing your feedback are those least likely to read it. Struggling students, especially, can have negative associations with teachers' marks on their work and avoid the risk of feeling yet worse about their performance.

Thoughtful feedback on student work can be highly valuable, but an overworked teacher might choose to use it selectively. In this case, add comments to student work only when they are most likely to be read and influence learning. For example:

- when reading the feedback is required for the next assignment, such as when comments on a first essay draft can help the student write the second essay draft
- when class time is set aside for students to read and consider feedback
- when students are permitted to use the feedback to improve assignment performance

- **Rethink how your time is best spent.** In a literature review based on more than 50,000 students and 800 meta-analyses, Hattie (2009) found homework's effect on student achievement is well below the average effect of innovations, meaning there are many more instructional endeavors that are more successful. Ask yourself which will most help students learn:

- teaching a stellar lesson that has students engaged, excited, and learning and using concepts at a higher level; or
- grading assignments

As Alber (2010) pointed out, it benefits students more for the teacher to devote time to planning dynamic lessons than it does to waste that time inputting every assignment in a gradebook. Take an honest look at your grading time and consider how much of it would be better spent lesson planning or recharging so you have more energy to devote to kids.

Teacher's Burnout Advice

"A third-grade teacher . . . helped me accept that I couldn't chase down every lesson idea or write sentences of explanation for each error. It gave me the freedom to focus on interaction with kids. That's made all the difference."

— *Sean McComb*
2014 National Teacher of
the Year (Gelman, 2015, p. 43)

- **Rethink homework as the primary means for providing feedback.** You may have heard the analogy that using formative data (that can influence what you're currently doing) is like operating on a live body, whereas using summative data (that is used to reflect on instruction after the fact) is like performing an autopsy.

Well, when your feedback is a day or more old, as is the case with most grading, you're more likely to be performing an autopsy rather than an operation. In other words, your feedback is less likely to impact students.

If homework is the main way in which you regularly let individual students know how they are doing in each content area (e.g., on each CCSS), you are likely not benefiting from tools that make it easier to give students effective feedback. For example, whiteboards and responders and data can allow you to give feedback to students instantly rather than waiting to return graded homework. See the "Technology" chapter in this book for details.

Change Your Approach to Grading

Now that you've critically reconsidered the value of grading, it should be easier to reevaluate your current grading practices. There are pros and cons to most of the upcoming strategies. If you are risking burnout, however, it is worth implementing changes that will keep you in a functional, low-stress state and free up your time for excellent lesson planning and other tasks that help kids. Apply these strategies as appropriate for your circumstances:

- **Rethink assignments.** If you send home one worksheet per night for each student in your class, or if you have students working on worksheets during class, you should explore some of the latest literature on assignments. For example, research flipped classrooms, maker spaces, project-based learning (PBL), and the term "rethinking homework."

  Often a move to higher rigor levels, better CCSS alignment, and more real-world applicability involves fewer "traditional" (e.g., question-and-answer) assignments. Even if your current assignments are rigorous and well aligned, which is likely, this shift can be a great thing for grading, as there can be fewer small details to check.

- **Use journals or portfolios in a new way.** Many teachers groan (as I used to) at the word "journal" or "portfolio," as they associate these terms with carting home boxes of work to power through every other week. If leveraged with an eye for ease, however, these formats can relieve teachers of grading time while remaining effective feedback tools for students.

  For example, students can compile less weighty assignments in a portfolio or journal that can be scored as a whole or within which you grade papers the students self-select as the best . . . or any other approach you develop that makes scores less cumbersome to determine.

If portfolios and their contents remain free of students' names (e.g., the name on the cover can be folded back and secured, or a student ID number can be used in its place), you can let students assign grades that you merely check and alter if necessary. For example, every 2 weeks, place desks (with students) in a circle around the room so they face away from one another. Hand one portfolio to each student (not his or her own) and let the child pick and score one paper within it. Use a student-friendly rubric that will lend graders the instructional benefit of evaluating to which practices the piece conforms.

> "There are advantages to being elected president. The day after I was elected, I had my high school grades classified top secret."
>
> — *Ronald Reagan*

Students who finish early can spend time adding comments to support the score. When students are finished, surprise them with how to pass the portfolios (e.g., "pass them three students to your left") or let them get up and move to new seats (e.g., "sit two desks to your right"). Let them score again. Continue until three assignments per portfolio are scored, and use the scores to assign a total. Peer grading is another way in which students can learn from one another while also better learning expectations (Alber, 2010).

Students can later challenge scores they were given if they disagree with them, though peer scoring works best for preliminary scores you then adjust as necessary. These scores need not go in the gradebook; they can be used to give students feedback, which is the main goal of a grade anyway. Remember that a score's role in supporting student learning is superior to its role in student grades.

- **Rely heavily on rubrics.** If an assignment is subjectively graded, it should have an accompanying rubric that uses student-friendly language. Unless the accompanying assignment is very basic, the rubric should have a separate column or row for each area in which the assignment is being scored (e.g., an essay rubric might have a column for grammar, a column for vocabulary, a column for style, and another column for organization).

While rubrics take extra time to develop, they save you time in the long run. For example:

  - Students (who should receive the rubric when they receive the assignment) have a better understanding of expectations, so they ask fewer questions and require less guidance (while simultaneously being empowered to produce better work).

- You can hand the rubric to volunteers you enlist to score the assignments on your behalf or use with peer scoring.

- By circling or otherwise indicating the score a student received in each area, you do not have to write out comments. Because each number value equates to a statement (e.g., 2 = paper lacked a thesis statement), the student already gets a slew of ready-made comments.

- The rubric can be used for future school years as well.

> "[My parents] wanted me to be a brain surgeon. I exceeded their expectations. I became a scholar and a teacher."
>
> — Harry Wong

Instead of a chart-format rubric, you might instead use a list of qualities or components that are required in an assignment. You can circle which aspects are present and use that number to total the student's score (or let a classroom volunteer do the totaling). Again, the student would automatically have a clear picture of what was present and what was missing. English teacher Jago (2005) adds that developing scoring rubrics as a department or grade level allows you to share the workload, build consensus, and develop a more well-rounded rubric.

- **Grade only part of each assignment.** Only score two to three carefully selected items or aspects on an assignment. Students will still need to complete the whole assignment in order to ensure good scores.

Some programs offer a formal approach to focus-area grading. For example, the John Collins Writing Workshop model (www.collinsed.com/fca.htm), allows you to pick one focus area per content category on which to focus. Students can even use a previously written piece to rewrite in order to meet the focus area requirements. This allows students to become intimately familiar with good writing practices while perfecting their craft, and it also allows you to streamline paper grading.

You can also take an informal approach to only grading part of each assignment. When it comes to writing, Cameron (2014) reminds fellow teachers not to grade aspects that will change with the second draft. For example, she explains if you encounter a weak thesis statement and/or introduction in a paper, you shouldn't grade the paragraph's grammar because it will change dramatically in the next draft anyway. Focus on just two main issues in a paper's first draft, and you can address other issues in subsequent drafts (Cameron, 2014).

Grade Type Definitions

- **Objectively Graded** questions or items are those that have a single, clear answer (as displayed on an answer key). E.g., the answer to Question 1 is "B" and no other answer is considered correct.

- **Subjectively Graded** questions, items, tasks, or projects are those for which the grader must judge which answers/responses/etc. are correct or what score(s) they should receive. E.g., scoring the essay involves using a rubric.

- **Don't do students' work for them.** Jago (2005) points out that comments about a sentence not making sense or a need to rephrase are more effective than actually rewriting a flawed sentence for a student. Just as it is counterproductive to do everything for a student while teaching him or her, you rob a student of the chance to work something out (thus authentically learning it) with more than a hint of guidance.

- **Rotate grading papers versus discussing papers with students.** Another strategy shared by Cameron (2014) works well with any subjectively graded (e.g., open-response) assignment. She recommends grading half of a stack of papers, then discussing the other half with students in person (after placing just a few bullet points on the back). Meet with those students one at a time for 5- to 10-minute meetings, and for the next essay you can swap which students get a grade versus a meeting (Cameron, 2014). Be sure you have an activity planned and/or a volunteer available that will allow you the time to meet with students in this way.

Delegate for Particular Grading Needs

Think of yourself like a CEO of grading. In a company, a CEO doesn't do everything herself or himself. Rather, he or she delegates so tasks less worthy of the CEO's expertise can be done by others. You can do the same with grading. For example, when a quiz has multiple-choice answers (as opposed to open response), it doesn't require a teacher's advanced schooling to determine if a student answered A for question 1 and B for question 2.

> ## Acquiring Student Help
>
> See the "Volume" chapter for details on how to acquire and make the most of student TAs or volunteers.

The following strategies can help you enlist the help of others to expedite grading practices when possible. Again, there are pros and cons to most of these strategies, but if you succumb to burnout, the consequences will be worse.

Reflect on your grading needs and distinguish between which items truly require your expertise and feedback. Determine which strategies will work with particular items you need graded and apply these strategies as appropriate for your circumstances:

- **Enlist student teaching assistants (TAs) for grading tasks.** Secondary students can often opt to serve as your TA during their elective periods, and elementary students can often help out after completing their work. The main concern when utilizing students' time, however, is that *you must ensure it is also quality learning time* for the students. For this reason, you should never ask students to grade multiple-choice work, which does not require much thought to grade. Rather, technology (covered later in this chapter) makes multiple-choice grading instant and easy. If you cannot defend the grading time in the same way you can defend the value of peer assessment, such as to a parent or a principal, then the child should not spend time on a grading project.

  In addition to helping you with interesting nongrading tasks, student TAs can serve as wonderful preliminary scorers of student work that needs to be judged subjectively. Subjectively assessing work relating to what the student TA is learning in another class can enlist evaluation skills (high on Bloom's Taxonomy of Educational Objectives) paired with appropriate curriculum content. This can be beneficial to the TA and speed your own follow-up scoring of the work, since you must determine the ultimate score. Again, the grading time must have educational benefit to the TA. Provide your TAs with student-friendly rubrics (e.g., simple language and clear examples) and train them how to use these rubrics to score student work. Also show your TAs sample student work (e.g., saved or copied from previous years, with names removed) that exemplify rubric categories. It's typically good practice to share these samples with your students prior to assignment completion as well. Grade some work together until you're sure your TA has the hang of it.

The scores your TAs assign can serve as preliminary scores that you check (and have the chance to alter) before finalizing scores. See the "Volume" chapter for help making the best use of student TAs and peer grading.

Peer-Assessment Tips

English teacher Jago (2005) notes a common pitfall to peer scoring (only the academically proficient students might score others' work appropriately) and offers these tips:

- Let peer scorers answer basic questions such as whether the work made sense, if they could follow the student's argument, and where the work got confusing.

- Pair scorers together, and do so conscientiously (e.g., boys with girls, no best-friend pairs, etc.).

- Have students read their drafts aloud to their partners and stop after each sentence to answer questions the partner has.

- **Let students peer assess and self-assess.** If you use well-crafted rubrics with student-friendly language and examples that clarify what to look for, students can do an effective job assessing others' (or their own) projects. This can be a preliminary step in grading (with you then checking papers and assigning the final grade), or it can work well with initial drafts until a final draft makes it to your grading stack. Student grading not only lessens the teacher's workload; it acquaints students with expectations and lets them learn from one another (Alber, 2010).

Acquiring Adult Help

See the "Volume" chapter for details on how to acquire adult volunteers and maximize their time.

However, be wary of impartial scoring. For example, you don't want one student being easy on another because the two are friends. Emphasizing the value of an honest critique can help, but problems can still arise. Consider having students place their student ID numbers on papers rather than their names and pass out papers randomly so no one knows who has one's paper (thus students won't feel others' prying eyes on them as they score).

- **Enlist adult volunteers for grading tasks.** This book's "Volume" chapter can help you secure the help of parent volunteers, community volunteers, teacher retiree volunteers, and student teachers for your classroom. These individuals can all help grade, particularly for preliminary grading tasks.

Special considerations for this help include:

- Adult volunteers can require just as much support as student graders, particularly if they have no teaching experience. As described earlier in the "Enlist student TAs for grading tasks" section, give volunteers clear rubrics and sample student work (to match rubric descriptions) when grading is subjective. Grade some work together until you're sure your volunteer has the hang of it.

- Parent volunteers might be overly lenient or overly hard on their own kids. If you teach multiple periods, consider not having parents score their own children's class periods. Otherwise, give volunteers' children's papers an especially close check afterward.

- You can take some liberties with adult volunteers that you can't with students. For example, you don't have to worry about the time being instructional, and adult volunteers can run errands and make photocopies.

See the "Volume" chapter for help acquiring and making the most of volunteers. The "Community Relations" chapter provides additional help.

Let Technology Help You

Unlock the power of technology . . . even if the mere thought makes you cringe. Imagine a farming community in which every farmer drove a tractor except one, who insisted on pushing a medieval plow because he or she was intimidated by learning to use the tractor. Imagine how far behind the plow pusher would fall. Teachers who don't make good use of technology are similar to the plow pusher. They are easily smart enough to master technology tools; they merely have to get over their reservations and put the initial time into learning.

The time technology saves you, particularly where grading is concerned, is simply too substantial to forgo. Technological tools require some of your time to learn, but the payoff in time savings is worth it.

The following strategies can help you use technology to make grading easier and less time consuming. The moment you suspect you might struggle with any of these strategies, arrange for help. For example, your school's technology coordinator

Tech Can Support Open Response

Don't mistake technology-based grading as an approach that doesn't support subjective grading (e.g., open-response questions, complex learning tasks, etc.), because it actually can support subjective grading very well. Multiple-choice questions and short-answer questions (e.g., where only a specific phrase is correct) can be automatically graded by technology. As for subjective grading, you can simply add your own manually inputted score to whatever form or interface is being used.

For example, imagine an assignment has five questions that are multiple choice or short answer, followed by five questions that are open response. Use technology to score the assignment's first five questions, then manually input the remaining five scores based on whatever judgment or rubric you are using. Depending on the technological approach (such as those described later in this section), you might bubble these manual scores on students' homework sheets before they are scanned, or you might type them onto a Google Form after students complete the assignment online, and so forth. Either way, the technology can automatically total the final scores for you, automatically import them into your gradebook, student and parent portal, progress reports, and the like. The "Technology" chapter offers details.

or computer science teacher might be able to assist you. If you contact your district office information technology (IT) Department, someone can often be sent to your classroom to help. Many students also make adept technology coaches. The point is: don't let frustration stand in your way of leveraging technology for grading. The "Improve Technology's Odds for Success" section of the "Technology" chapter can help you secure the help you need. Apply these strategies as appropriate for your circumstances:

- **Use webcam grading for assignments and assessments.** You can use an ordinary webcam to instantly score assignments and assessments. Imagine this:
  - As students enter the classroom, they drop homework in a tray. Any of their multiple-choice answers are instantly and automatically scored (literally just by landing in the tray), a computer screen shows students how they performed, and the scores are instantly and automatically loaded into your gradebook. You can instantly see how the class performed and group students based on their needs for the day's lesson.

- As students finish an assessment, they drop it in a tray. Any of their multiple-choice answers are instantly and automatically scored (literally just by landing in the tray), a computer screen shows students how they performed, and students can move to an appropriate station based on this score to do appropriate follow-up work (or get an appropriate follow-up assignment). Scores are instantly and automatically loaded into your gradebook, and you can instantly see how the class performed, see individual students' and student groups' needs, and so on.

- You can bubble subjectively graded scores (e.g., rubric based, or judging right versus wrong yourself) afterward, and these can be added (e.g., scanned or inputted) just as easily, at which point they are instantly and automatically loaded into your gradebook, and so forth.

You might also opt to randomly pass out papers right after multiple-choice answers are scored (e.g., if students bubble their ID numbers on their sheets but do not include their names on assignments). You can let students peer-assess remaining answers. Simply go over possible answers and/or a related rubric and allow students to bubble a score for the paper they are grading. You can even pair students so that two students score two students' answers.

Note this approach is only an option if evaluating and scoring one another's work doubles as a worthwhile learning activity for students. This will depend on what students are evaluating and how they are being guided in its evaluation. Students can later be responsible for challenging scores they were given if they disagree with them, though peer scoring works best for preliminary scores you then adjust as necessary.

Not only can the scores automatically populate your gradebook, but they can also automatically populate your student and parent portal, progress reports, report cards, etc. If your district does not use products integrated to make this possible, it is worth advocating for better tools. See the "Technology" chapter to learn how you can make the above scenario (concerning webcam grading in the classroom) happen.

- **Use an online system for the automatic grading of assignments or assessments.** You can even use tools that cost you nothing to do this. Imagine this:

  - Students answer questions and/or respond to prompts online.

  - You don't have to pass out or collect any papers.

  - All responses appropriate for objective grading (e.g., multiple-choice answers or specific-term answers) are instantly graded.

- Students instantly get their own scores.

- You instantly get all students' scores, and these can automatically (and instantly) populate your gradebook (as well as other data systems).

- You can enter subjectively graded scores (e.g., for open response questions) later, at which point students' scores will automatically (and instantly) update in the data system, student and parent portal, progress reports, report cards, transcripts, and the like . . . on any synced data system the scores impact.

- Even if the entire assignment or assessment is subjectively graded, entering scores online calculates totals for you and puts them in appropriate places without additional labor on your part.

For example, teacher Pinelli (2015) had students complete a five-question online assessment as homework or in class after a lesson, then used the instant data to plan for the next day, allotting time based on commonly selected incorrect answers and arranging differentiation for individuals or student groups ahead of time. See the "Technology" chapter to learn how you can make the above scenario happen. In addition, the "Environment" chapter can help you set up your classroom for easy differentiation.

Online Scoring for Writing

English teacher Jago (2005) notes how advanced computer scoring processes have become for student writing samples (at least as a preliminary score to cover aspects like mechanics) and suggests:

- Educational Testing Service (ETS) Criterion® Online Writing Evaluation Service www.ets.org/criterion/about

- **Use "clickers" for assignments and tests.** "Clickers" go by many names: classroom response systems (CRSs), handheld responders, or merely apps that provide the same function and can be used on any web-enabled device (e.g., iPhones, iPads, etc.). Basically, clickers allow you to pose questions to a class of students, who then click their answers on their clicker devices. You then get immediate access to the response data, so you can see what percentage of students answered in each way (e.g., 35% of students knew A was the answer, but 42% thought B was the answer).

Clickers can also be used to let students answer questions anonymously (e.g., 22% of students understand the concept and are ready to move on, but 78% require more explanation and/or time). See the "Technology" chapter to learn how you can use clickers to easily acquire students' answers.

- **Use an online gradebook.** If you hand write and hand calculate scores in a written gradebook, this practice needs to stop. It is simply too time consuming a process for a professional like you to continue. See the "Technology" chapter to learn how you can use an online gradebook to make your life far easier.

Reflection Exercises

The following items can be answered individually and/or discussed as a group.

1. Explain three ways in which graded assignments (and the comments teachers write on such assignments) are limited in their abilities to impact students' learning.
   A. _____
   _____
   _____
   B. _____
   _____
   _____
   C. _____
   _____
   _____

2. Identify and describe items you spend the most time grading.
   _____
   _____
   _____
   _____

3. Describe three systems you will employ to reduce time spent grading. Be specific in the items being graded, the technology used, details you'll consider to make the systems successful, etc.
   A. _____
   _____
   _____

B. _____
_____
_____
C. _____
_____
_____

4. Describe a new means you'll employ to provide students with feedback that is immediate and meaningful.
_____
_____
_____
_____
_____

5. Pick a new technology you will use to automate (and thus reduce your time needed for) the grading of some assignments. Answer the following questions about this arrangement:
What is the technology? _____
_____

Where/how will you acquire it? _____
_____
_____

How will its use solve a specific problem and/or support student learning?
_____
_____

In what specific way will you use the technology in your classroom?
_____
_____
_____
_____

References

Alber, R. (2010, January 5). Tactics for tackling the grading dilemma. *Edutopia*. Retrieved from http://www.edutopia.org/grading-dilemma-strategies-tactics

Cameron, K. (2014, November 14). 5 ways to take the grind out of grading papers. *Classroom 2.0*. Retrieved from http://www.classroom20.com/forum/topics/5-ways-to-take-the-grind-out-of-grading-papers-1

Darling-Hammond, L. (2014, June 30). To close the achievement gap, we need to close the teaching gap. *Huffington Post*. Retrieved from http://www.huffingtonpost.com/linda-darlinghammond/to-close-the-achievement_b_5542614.html

Gelman, G. (2015, February). Art of living: The best advice I ever got. *Readers Digest, 185*(1107), 41–47. White Plains: NY: The Readers Digest Association.

Hattie, J. A. C. (2009). *Visibly learning from reports: The validity of score reports*. Paper presented at the annual meeting of the National Council for Measurement in Education (NCME). New York, NY: Routledge Taylor & Francis Group.

Jago, C. (2005). *Papers, papers, papers: An English teacher's survival guide*. Portsmouth, NH: Heinemann.

Krantz-Kent, R. (2008, March). Teachers' work patterns: When, where, and how much do U.S. teachers work? *Monthly Labor Review*, 52–59. Washington, DC: U.S. Department of Labor, Bureau of Labor Statistics.

Passarella, E. (2015). Do kids really need homework? *Real Simple, 11*, 150–151.

Pinelli, P. (2015, April 2). 6 reasons it's important to create your own online assessments. *eSchool News*. Retrieved from http://www.eschoolnews.com/2015/04/02/creating-online-assessments-431/?ps=drjrankin@gmail.com-001a000001JOTLm-003a000001g6MmL

Volume

"I Can Do Everything I Want, in Just 48 Hours per Day"

Teacher Confession: "I enjoy the work I do, I just wish there weren't so much of it. It's gotten to the point where I don't have a healthy amount of time for my family or for sleep. I love the work I'm producing—it's top notch and interesting—but I wish it didn't take so much time."

— *Rush A. Round*

Work overload is one of the primary factors that creates burnout at work (Maslach & Leiter, 2008; Skovholt & Trotter-Mathison, 2011). In a similar vein, "time pressure" was indicated as the number-one everyday stressor by the more than 30,000 teachers surveyed, with 47% of teachers (and 58% of teachers who report being often stressed) reporting this as a daily contributor to stress (American Federation of Teachers, 2015).

Not only can doing too much sour your mood, it can significantly reduce your effectiveness. Stressed, overworked teachers can develop a condition neuroscientists call executive function overload, during which the overstimulated brain becomes unable to think clearly or register emotions (Strauss, 2014).

Sometimes external factors are largely responsible for a teacher's work overload. For example, a class schedule that doesn't include a planning period or an administrator who makes superfluous demands can promote the piling up of work. However, even when external demands bear some of the blame, there are often ways in which teachers' own practices result in unnecessary work. While the "Overcommitting" and "Administration" chapters will help you prevent others from burying you in work, this chapter will help you avoid adding to the pile.

> "For fast-acting relief, try slowing down."
>
> — *Lily Tomlin*

The UK Department for Education's Teachers' Workload Diary Survey indicated UK teachers work more than 50 hours a week; 55% of teachers reported some of their time was spent on unnecessary or bureaucratic tasks, and 45% reported this had increased from the year before (Stanley, 2014). Teachers in other countries mirror this.

Taking a step back to assess what is most important and then letting go of less important tasks (e.g., don't grade every assignment) can help alleviate teacher burnout (Warren, 2014). Renowned teacher Vicki Davis (2014) lists choosing what to overlook as one of the top 12 ways to fend off burnout, as trying to be perfect is a hindrance. For example, her kids are happier eating frozen lasagna served by a happy mother than they would be if she served a home-cooked meal in a foul mood. There are ways you can reduce your own workload at school.

Prime Your Outlook

You probably deserve an award. If you're the sort of teacher who always tries to do more and always tries to do everything well (common personality traits of the overworked teacher), you deserve great gratitude, respect, and perhaps a standing ovation . . . and since you probably wouldn't be working so hard without the sole goal of helping kids, you probably don't care much about awards and recognition; you just care about your impact on students.

That's a great starting point for this section. If the priority is helping students, we can get rid of anything that doesn't effectively but also *efficiently* help kids. After all, if you're burned out, you actually become a less effective teacher.

The following strategies can help you make mindset adjustments to pave the way for reduced workload. Apply these strategies as appropriate for your circumstances:

- **Let go of perfectionism.** Unreasonable self-expectations can make a significant contribution to burnout, such as is often the case with child welfare workers (Van Hook & Rothenberg, 2009). Special education teacher Lori Smock says, "accepting less than perfection" is one of the top ways she avoids burnout, remembering she can always aim to do something better in the future if time will allow.

Of all the strategies in this book, this is one I struggle with the most. To keep myself in check, I have to catch myself when I'm caring too much about minute details and then talk myself down to a more lenient mindset.

Think critically about whether perfectionism is one of your personal struggles. Identify times or areas where you put more energy into finessing a project than was absolutely required.

> "Have no fear of perfection—you'll never reach it."
> — *Salvador Dali*

If you struggle with excessive expectations, vow to fight your perfectionist tendencies. If necessary, put a reminder in a spot you see every day. For example, tape "It doesn't have to be perfect" above your computer monitor, or change your laptop password to "Not2Perfect."

- **Set realistic goals each day.** Goal setting and time management can help prevent and alleviate burnout, as has been found to be the case with nurses who care for others (Demir, Ulusoy, & Ulusoy, 2003; Espeland, 2006). The to-do list tips in the "Overstimulation" chapter can help with this.

Treat yourself gently when determining what you will accomplish each day and each evening. Set expectations that are reasonable to accomplish, and maintain this threshold for what you will do. Sharing your goal with your partner or family can help you stick to your goal (though con-

> "I love when I teach my son a good lesson. But I love it even more when he teaches me."
> — *Brad Meltzer*

sider this carefully, as some loved ones are prone to going overboard and exacerbating stress). Though exceptions may occasionally arise, try your best to stick to the limits you establish. Meanwhile, you can pursue other strategies in this book to reduce workload and prevent work from piling up.

Prioritize and Purge in Multiple Areas

I love to throw parties. I get accolades for how beautiful everything looks and how smoothly things run. Yet it's always a huge time commitment to prepare. My husband asked me, "What would happen if you didn't post signs for the restrooms?" His barely suppressed smile gave away his meaning. In my effort to accommodate any need that might arise during the party, I was wasting time on details that weren't essential. Sure, the bathrooms

> **Q:** Why did the teacher let the student crumple up the teacher's paper?
> **A:** The paper listed the teacher's New Year's resolutions.

signs were helpful for people, but guests wouldn't wet themselves without the signs; they'd simply ask someone for directions or find a bathroom on their own.

The issue of doing nonessential tasks faces many teachers. This problem is compounded by the fact that teachers do so much in so many areas already. For example, every lesson created is an opportunity to go overboard, so daily lesson creation means daily chances to overdo . . . and that's in just one area of a teacher's daily responsibilities.

The following strategies can help you prioritize tasks and purge those that are nonessential. Apply these strategies as appropriate for your circumstances:

- **Look to the content standards you teach.** Reflecting on whatever you specifically set out to teach in your particular classroom helps you focus on what matters most in achieving your instructional goals. Consult your standards and pacing guides, and scrutinize how your lessons lead students to mastery of those standards. If you do not teach a core subject or are unsure what standards you should be teaching, check with your administration or with staff who offer related expertise.

  During my first year as a teacher, I made the mistake of following a colleague's direction to model my lessons after the textbook's content. When I looked closely at the standards (well into the school year, sadly), I realized I had been teaching lots of content I didn't have to teach. What a waste of time for me and—more importantly—for my students.

  Prior to CCSS, textbooks were typically marketed across the country and annotated with standard-alignment after-the-fact (e.g., the book showed Iowa's standards in the margin when sold in Iowa, Ohio's standards in the book's pamphlet companion when the book was sold in Ohio, etc.). In other words, to save money, publishers would write one textbook and then sell that same book to each state as if it was aligned to that state's standards. Because the same book was meant to accommodate all states' standards, there was far more in a textbook than a teacher should (or could) teach.

  Even where common standards have arrived, many publishers have tried to save money by taking their old materials and trying to squeeze them into CCSS alignment. Basically, there is far more content in most "CCSS-aligned" products than you really need to be teaching. For example:

  - In a review of "Common Core–aligned" K–8 math instructional materials, 85% of the series failed to truly be aligned to CCSS (Heitin, 2015).

  - When Denver Public Schools reviewed "Common Core–aligned" textbooks and curriculum on the market for math and English, none were found to meet the district's needs, particularly considering the needs of English learners (Zubrzycki, 2014).

- The developers of the Next-Generation Science Standards (NGSS) report there are not many NGSS–aligned materials available and won't be for some time (Roseman & Koppal, 2015). Some developers and publishers claim their materials are NGSS aligned even though the materials were developed for older standards (Roseman & Koppal, 2015).

- In 2013, only 44% of middle school social studies teachers found their digital instructional resources to be sufficient; this has grown to 64%, but gaps at all secondary grades—for example, CCSSs that simply aren't covered— are still rampant (Bill and Melinda Gates Foundation, 2015).

In non–CCSS states, acquiring materials meant for custom standards is even more difficult. If you encounter lessons that don't support the standards, they are likely not worth keeping. Note there are exceptions, such as lessons that support organizational skills or character development; exceptions should be conscientiously made.

- **Determine what can go.** Think of the types of work projects (e.g., assignments you build, lesson plans you write, etc.) that require the most work on your part. Consider these first for possible elimination or replacement then consider the rest of your workload. Ask yourself the questions in Figure 6.1 of each work project and respond accordingly.

- **Prioritize and determine what is optional.** When faced with an insurmountable workload, one can only do one's best. Determine which tasks are most important, do those first, and consider letting other tasks go. For example, if you are developing new lesson plans and typically write your own exercises to use as prelesson warm-ups with students, consider using already-developed exercises in the textbook. Then you can wait to write your own exercises when you teach next year without the burden of developing the whole lesson from scratch.

- **Rework cumbersome habits or processes.** It is an advantage to teach (particularly the same content) year after year, as you can streamline and fine-tune almost everything you do. Take a critical look at your habits and processes, particularly those that occur frequently, such as a daily routine. Consider how these can be modified, replaced, or eliminated for improved efficiency. Then make warranted changes. See Table 6.1 for examples.

- **Foresee and avoid drama.** In a school setting, prioritization extends to choosing battles, as teachers should only fight for what matters most if they are to avoid burnout (Davis, 2014). Before challenging an administrator or confronting a

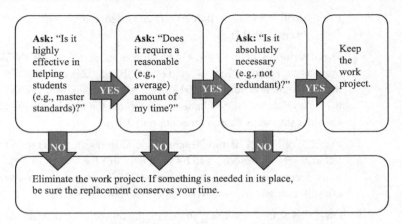

Figure 6.1 How to Determine Which Work Projects to Eliminate

Other Factors

- If **grading** is one of your biggest time hogs, see the "Grading" chapter for help.

- If you're overwhelmed by the number of lesson plans or **projects** you must create to meet students' needs, see the "Curriculum" chapter for help.

- If **others** are bloating your work volume, such as administrator or district office requests, see the "Overcommitting" and "Administration" chapters for help.

colleague, consider (a) what the worst-case ramifications could be and (b) whether these ramifications would be worth your effort. If the drain on your time and emotions would be detrimental, save your effort for a future problem or speak out anonymously.

For example, you can always mail an anonymous note to your administrators to make them aware of an important problem if you just can't spare the time to focus on it at length. While face-to-face communication is best for promoting positive relations with administration, battling burnout is an emergency situation that lends you allowances when you aren't in a position to handle something negative and consuming.

Table 6.1 Examples of Burdens With Possible Solutions

Identified Burden	Solution
Rush creates a finished sample of each history project (e.g., battle scene diorama with causes and effects/actions annotated) to be able to show students before they build their own.	*Modify* When students finish the project, Rush keeps examples (with students' consent) to serve as samples for the next year. To compensate during the initial year, he does his best to be descriptive, and he provides incentive for early turn-in to be able to show finished projects to those still working.
Rush prints each lesson, hole-punches it, and stores it in a binder on the staff lounge shelves where other teachers can use it.	*Replace* Rush no longer maintains lesson binders. Instead, he houses his lessons in the district's learning management system (LMS). This way all teachers can instantly access them (or he can control access) without Rush having to take added steps.
After Rush teaches a lesson, he types a reflection (on how the lesson went) and adds it to his lesson plan document. That way he can read and consider it next year.	*Eliminate* Rush still reflects, but he doesn't type it. He already makes any needed edits to the lesson (e.g., 5 fewer minutes for the introduction and 5 more minutes for students' hands-on time), so those changes already account for virtually everything the reflection would have to offer when Rush teaches the same lesson next year.

Leverage Resources

You can further lighten your workload by pushing for better resources and making the most of resources you already have. Such resources might be technology, time, curriculum, online resources, or other forms of support.

The following strategies can help you acquire and maximize resources that help you minimize workload. Apply these strategies as appropriate for your circumstances:

- **Start with existing lessons.** Abundant resources, many of them free and online, can reduce the need for you to create lessons and their components (e.g., warm-up prompts, quizzes, handouts, etc.) from scratch. The "Curriculum" chapter can help you leverage resources to significantly cut lesson plan development. For example, the chapter will help you use online tools and technology like a curriculum management system (CMS) and advocate for the adoption of better curriculum. Whether you use an existing lesson "as is" or tweak it, it will typically take less time than creating a whole lesson from scratch.

- **Use technology to go paperless.** Paper use means having to print things, copy things, pass things out, run to the copy room when you're short on things, file things, throw things out, return things to students . . . that's a lot of work, and much of it is unnecessary. See the "Technology" chapter for help with tools that enable you to go paperless when appropriate.

- **Advocate for more time.** Time is a blessed resource when it comes to managing work volume. The more time you have, the more you're able to tackle (and thus reduce remaining) workload.

Teachers are particularly strapped for time if they don't have a designated planning period or if their planning period is routinely monopolized by campus endeavors like PD or professional learning community (PLC) meetings. If you don't have adequate planning time, request it.

Whether or not you have official planning time, you might consider asking for isolated blocks of time. For example, if you are developing all of your department's unit quizzes (which, despite best practices for collaboration, can happen), you might ask your principal to provide a substitute to cover your class for a day. He or she might deem the cost worthy of the return, and you could pick a day least likely to hurt your students (like a testing day or tech lab day), when you won't be as missed.

Teachers who regularly carry the bulk of a department's burden might even ask for an additional planning period. For example, imagine your district has mandated regular, formal assessment (e.g., weekly diagnostic quizzes), and you and a colleague are collaboratively building all of your department's tests (which the department's other teachers then critique and request changes to). Your administration should understand the added workload, its necessity, and its value (e.g., imagine you and your colleague are trained experts in assessment writing and there isn't time for all department members to be involved in the initial draft). Whereas giving every teacher on campus a second planning period would be out of the question, your principal might deem extra planning for one or two of you worthwhile. He or she might alternatively consider a roving planning period that goes to a different teacher each week when that teacher assumes a project's roving role.

Get Helpers for Your Classroom

While trying to lessen your workload, you can also increase the number of hands helping you tackle it. If you get creative, you can find all sorts of volunteers.

The following strategies can help you find classroom volunteers and put them to work. Apply these strategies as appropriate for your circumstances:

- **Recruit adults as volunteers.** Please see the "Get Adults Involved in Your Classroom" section of the "Community Relations" chapter of this book. Tips are provided for securing the help of parents, family members, retirees (like retired teachers), student teachers, and other community members.

- **Recruit your own students as TAs and volunteers.** I love student helpers. They are often more enthusiastic than adults and sometimes more effective. Secondary students can often opt to serve as your TAs during their elective periods, and elementary students can often help out after completing their work.

Working With Student Helpers

See the "Grading" chapter for guidance in how student helpers' time might be spent, how to make this quality learning time, and what support these students might require.

However, student helpers require added caution. Your priority when utilizing students' time is that *you must ensure it is also quality learning time for the students*. See the "Grading" chapter for guidelines in this area, such as sparing students from mindless, multiple-choice grading and instead giving them more challenging, learning-focused tasks.

- **Recruit other teachers' students as volunteers.** I got so good at utilizing kid volunteers that students would randomly show up at my classroom to help (they had finished their classwork early and their teachers had sent them over). I don't know how I would have survived without them, and they loved being useful rather than bored.

Elementary teachers' students from other classes might finish early, ready for a new challenge, without their teachers being prepared to engage them with an added, worthwhile task. Secondary teachers of Leadership, Associated Student Body (ASB), Peer Assistance & Leadership (PAL), and other courses where project demands fluctuate can have any number of students anxious to help but not enough work to give them on a particular day. Other teachers' TAs are often left without enough worthwhile work, as well.

Let your fellow teachers know you are always happy to engage these students in tasks that interest and challenge them, whether it involves honing their organizational skills or practicing their content area skills using a rubric to evaluate student work for preliminary scores. Then be ready to put these students to work (see the next section).

Make the Most of Helpers' Time

Volunteers are precious, and teachers should make good use of their time. The following strategies can help you maximize times when you have classroom helpers. Apply these strategies as appropriate for your circumstances:

- **Be ready for volunteers' arrival.** Being well prepared and making smart decisions about task allocation is vital to getting the most out of volunteers. As tasks come up that are appropriate for volunteers to do instead of you, have an established place and way to set aside these tasks. Include everything volunteers will need to accomplish these tasks. For example:
  - a place to sit at a table or desk
  - supplies (pens, paperclips, gradebook entry forms rather than direct access, etc.)
  - papers clearly labeled (like a "to grade" tray and a "graded" tray, with a scoring form paperclipped to each set of papers with which it belongs)
  - one- to five-step directions, printed large and bold where they won't be missed, clarifying the basics of a task (e.g., if you always have items in the "graded" tray that have to be scored in a particular way); these directions will reinforce verbal directions you give and can be saved (with assignments or assessments) for next year so any time putting together special directions isn't wasted
  - backup tasks you won't need for some time, so helpers are never left with nothing to do; for adults it might be a project like reorganizing a corner cabinet; for students it might be a teachers' edition textbook chapter secured with a copy of the form on the upcoming page.
  - student-friendly rubrics (e.g., simple language and clear examples)

Help Me Design a Lesson   Your name: _____

Lesson: I plan to teach:

Directions: Think of a great way to teach this lesson. The activity should:
● really help kids learn the lesson
● have every kid involved ("hands on")
● be fun for kids

Write your ideas here:

Bonus: After copying this page, use the back of this sheet or extra paper to add details. For example, what questions or sample problems (with answers) should students get as a warm-up activity? If your idea involves a game, what should be written on the game pieces? **Thank you!**

- sample student work (e.g., saved or copied from previous years, with names removed) that exemplify rubric categories

When your systems are consistent, helpers can get used to these systems and require less guidance when helping in the future. See the "Grading" chapter for help regarding appropriate tasks for student helpers, who can often do more than adults might initially think.

- **Maximize volunteers' help time.** Be ready for volunteers' arrival, and establish a routine for their involvement that discourages volunteers from interrupting you. Over time, you will get better and better at setting aside tasks that can be handled by volunteers. WeAreTeachers and Volunteer Spot (2013), which reported 48% of teachers struggle finding time to prepare activities for volunteers, suggested assigning the same assignment to the same volunteer each time or designating a parent leader as the one who assigns tasks to other volunteers.

Get to know (and apply) volunteers' specialties. For example:

- Bilingual adults and students alike can translate your classroom communications (nothing student specific) to be sent home or posted to an online portal.

- Student graduates of tech classes can tackle tech tasks, such as fixing your jammed printer or helping out during their tech period when your students are all on laptops or using handheld devices.

  According to a thousand-participant survey by WeAreTeachers and Volunteer Spot (2013), 50% of teachers need help with computer skills, 45% with designing newsletters, 44% with gardening, and 43% with career readiness information. For such needs, there is a potential volunteer with the skills to help.

- Adults can circulate and assist struggling students, as can academically proficient students as long as it will reinforce their own learning and no student is chronically in this role.

- While retired teachers and student teachers can write adept lessons, don't overlook students for parts of this task. Give students a specific lesson portion you haven't yet created and have them brainstorm on ways to teach the content using the form on the previous page. Their original ideas might surprise and help you, classes love hearing a lesson was a student's invention, and devising how to teach something can help students learn the concept themselves.

If you provide older volunteers with Internet access (with adult content blocked for student users), you can task volunteers with finding and bookmarking lessons or lesson portions that best teach a particular content standard. You can give volunteers the OERs list in the "Curriculum" chapter to get them started. Then, when you sit down to find lessons for that standard, you can start with the volunteers' recommendations to save time.

- **Consider student privacy.** Parent and student volunteers should not have access to other students' personal matters. For this reason, you should not ask these volunteers to translate a letter home to specific parents about their children. Likewise, the volunteers should never use a computerized data system containing information on performance, contact information, or demographics.

  You might also consider asking students to use their school ID numbers rather than names on their papers (be sure to first consider how this will impact passing papers back to students). The "Technology" chapter's tips on scanning and on going paperless (such as using Google Forms to submit assignment responses) can make nameless papers a more viable option.

- **Thank all helpers profusely.** Whether your helper is a student or an adult, let them bask in your gratitude. This is especially important for students' self-esteem and character development. Plus, you will likely get more time and effort from your volunteers, and they will often recruit even more volunteers to your cause. Some ideas from Bantuveris (2013) include sending parents student-created thank-you cards or posting a short video or photo on class websites. Just remember to pick thanks-giving methods you find to be fast and easy.

Reflection Exercises

The following items can be answered individually and/or discussed as a group.

1. How many hours per week maximum, outside of your official work hours, can you comfortably devote to work? This should be a limitation that allows you time for loved ones and time for yourself (e.g., exercise, hobbies, and quiet time). _____

2. Using Figure 6.1, evaluate the lessons and lesson components you currently use with your students. Based on this assessment, which items will you eliminate, modify, or replace for upcoming instruction (this can be for the current and/or upcoming school year)?

_____
_____
_____
_____
_____

3. Identify a routine or process in your classroom that is more cumbersome than it ought to be. Develop a new process (to replace the old) that is more efficient and makes adequate use of available technology. Describe the improved process.

_____
_____
_____
_____
_____

4. List three resources that will help you reduce or manage work volume.

A. _____
_____
B. _____
_____
C. _____
_____

5. Pick two kinds of helpers you will enlist to help you with your workload. Answer the following questions for each of these.
What kind of helper will you enlist?

A. _____ B. _____

How, specifically, will you recruit this helper's help? Peek at the "Community Relations" chapter if necessary.

A. _____ B. _____

_____ _____
_____ _____
_____ _____

How will you prepare for this helper in order to make best use of his or her time?

A. _____ B. _____

_____ _____

_____ _____

_____ _____

With what kind of tasks will this helper help?

A. _____ B. _____

_____ _____

_____ _____

_____ _____

6. What steps will you take to ensure student privacy when your helper is interacting with student work or near student information?

_____

_____

_____

_____

References

American Federation of Teachers. (2015). *Quality of worklife survey*. Retrieved from http://www.aft.org/sites/default/files/worklifesurveyresults2015.pdf

Bantuveris, K. (2013, September 13). 5 tips for engaging parent volunteers in the classroom. *Edutopia*. Retrieved from http://www.edutopia.org/blog/strategies-for-engaging-parent-volunteers-karen-bantuveris

Bill and Melinda Gates Foundation. (2015). *Teachers know best: What teachers want from digital instructional tools 2.0*. Retrieved from http://collegeready.gatesfoundation.org/wp-content/uploads/2015/11/TeacherKnowBest-2.0.pdf

Davis, V. (2014, May 20). 12 choices to help you step back from burnout. *Edutopia*. Retrieved from http://www.edutopia.org/blog/12-choices-step-back-from-burnout-vicki-davis?utm_source=SilverpopMailing&utm_medium=email&utm_campaign=022515%20enews-A%20sm%20gm&utm_content=&utm_term=blog1&spMailingID=10733072&spUserID=MzgwNjgyODYwNjUS1&spJobID=481863955&spReportId=NDgxODYzOTU1S0

Demir, A., Ulusoy, M., & Ulusoy, M. F. (2003). Investigation of factors influencing burnout levels in the professional and private lives of nurses. *International Journal of Nursing Studies, 40*(8), 807–827.

Espeland, K. E. (2006). Overcoming burnout: How to revitalize your career. *The Journal of Continuing Education in Nursing, 37*(4), 178–184.

Heitin, L. (2015). Most math curricula found to be out of sync with Common Core. *Education Week.* Retrieved from http://www.edweek.org/ew/articles/2015/03/04/most-math-curricula-found-to-be-out.html?cmp=ENL-CM-NEWS1

Maslach, C., & Leiter, M. P. (2008). Early predictors of job burnout and engagement. *Journal of Applied Psychology, 93*(3), 498–512. doi: 10.1037/0021–9010.93.3.498

Roseman, J. E., & Koppal, M. (2015, January). Aligned or not? *Educational Leadership, 72*(4), 24–27. Alexandria, VA: ASCD.

Skovholt, T. M., & Trotter-Mathison, M. J. (2011). *The resilient practitioner: Burnout prevention and self-care strategies for counselors, therapists, teachers, and health professionals* (2nd ed.). New York, NY: Routledge, Taylor and Francis Group, LLC.

Stanley, J. (2014, October 13). How unsustainable workloads are destroying the quality of teaching. *Schools Week.* Retrieved from http://schoolsweek.co.uk/how-unsustainable-workloads-are-destroying-the-quality-of-teaching

Strauss, V. (2014, December 12). Teacher: The day I knew for sure I was burned out. *The Washington Post.* Retrieved from http://www.washingtonpost.com/blogs/answer-sheet/wp/2014/12/12/teacher-the-day-i-knew-for-sure-i-was-burned-out/?utm_content=buffer993c8&utm_medium=social&utm_source=twitter.com&utm_campaign=buffer

Van Hook, M. P., & Rothenberg, M. (2009). Quality of life and compassion satisfaction/fatigue and burnout in child welfare workers: A study of the child welfare workers in community based care organizations in central Florida. *Social Work and Christianity, 36*(1), 36–54.

Warren, F. (2014, May 29). Teacher burnout is real 4 ways to avoid it. *The Huffington Post.* Retrieved from http://www.huffingtonpost.com/franchesca-warren/teacher-burnout_b_5401551.html

WeAreTeachers & Volunteer Spot. (2013). *Parent volunteers in the classroom.* Retrieved from http://www.volunteerspot.com/Parents-Volunteer-In-The-Classroom

Zubrzycki, J. (2014, December 17). *Denver public schools "back to the drawing board" in search for common core-aligned curriculum.* Retrieved from http://co.chalkbeat.org/2014/12/17/denver-public-schools-back-to-the-drawing-board-in-search-for-common-core-aligned-curriculum/#.VP3g2_nF-So

7

Overcommitting
"I'm My School's 'Go-to' Volunteer"

Teacher Confession: "Our teachers are great teachers, but not everyone steps up to help outside of the classroom. There're a handful of us the principal goes to when she needs 'hands on deck,' because she knows we'll get the job done. Whether it's running the homework lab, showing up for a board meeting, or chaperoning the afterschool dance, we ladies (plus Phil, the lone man in the group) get it all done. If we didn't, who would? Our kids and principal need us."
— *Linda Hand*

Teacher Confession: "I don't look like a burnt out teacher. My classes run smoothly, my students do great, and I'm the kind of teacher other teachers come to for advice. I like being the teacher who has it all together, and I like being a teacher our principal turns to for support. But I'm having a really hard time keeping everything up. I picture a house of cards tumbling down when my fuel runs out. I dread that day."
— *Lynn Mia Near*

Teachers are so eager to make a difference that they can be their own worst enemy in causing their own burnout (Neufeldnov, 2014). One of the primary hazards for burnout is an inability to say no, also known as the treadmill effect or heroic syndrome (Skovholt & Trotter-Mathison, 2011).

For example, in a study of 1,699 primary school teachers in Turkey, those who devoted added efforts to helping colleagues and the organization as a whole improved the environment, yet often at the cost of emotional exhaustion, which contributes to burnout (Inandi Buyukozkan, 2013). If you feel like Linda Hand, or if you find yourself juggling too many "added" jobs like she did, you could benefit from using the word "no."

> ## *Hear from a Principal*
>
> "The last thing I want is to burn out my staff. Unfortunately, offering students the full spectrum of an enriching education requires volunteers to function. So as long as I'm principal, I'll be asking for volunteers.
>
> I go first to those most likely to help, but I'm not psychic—I don't know who I'm burdening if teachers don't tell me. I'm juggling so much, I'm sure I even overlook some signals teachers give me.
>
> I need to be straight-up told, 'I'm too overwhelmed to help this time.' Then I'll find someone else. No hard feelings here."
>
> — *Jess Telmy**
>
> * not the principal's real name

Teacher A: How do you keep up with all this work? Do you multitask?
Teacher B: No, that's too slow. I centupletask.

This chapter is not meant to undermine a collaborative school culture in which—as Principal Jess Telmy notes—volunteering is fundamental to a school's ability to offer students the full spectrum of an enriching education. Teachers must be willing to lend extra hands at times when it is in students' best interest. However, this chapter is meant to prevent teachers assuming a larger volunteer role than their peers and to stop their volunteerism from undercutting their happiness.

Set Yourself Up for Success

One of the best ways to guard against burnout is to learn to set boundaries, such as by saying no to demanding requests (Skovholt & Trotter-Mathison, 2011). If you found it easy to say no, however, you would not struggle with this chapter's problem.

The following strategies can make it easier for you to turn down onerous requests for your time and help. Apply these strategies as appropriate for your circumstances:

- **Preconceive a "no" statement you find comfortable.** Devising and practicing a way to say no can help ease awkwardness you might feel when the time comes to say it. If a simple "no" is hard for you to say, you might prefer one of these phrases:

- "I wish I could say yes, but I've been very overwhelmed lately with work and definitely need to cut back on my commitments."

- "Regretfully, I'm too overextended to say yes. Have you considered . . ."

- "I'm so sorry, but I definitely have to say no. I've been particularly stressed lately, and I have to start scaling back on extra obligations."

Notice each response shows consideration, is firm, and provides a valid reason. Notice the reason is not restricted to only one request; rather, it could also stave off additional requests in the near future. Determine a response that works well for you, and try to recall it when needed.

- **Require time to think if you need it.** If, despite your planning, you find yourself about to cave in with a "yes," stop yourself by requesting time to think about your answer. Then return with a firm "no" within an hour (you don't want to keep others hanging). It is ideal to give your answer right away rather than waiting, but this approach is better than agreeing to something you need to forego.

- **Determine when a "yes" is OK.** An effective school work environment is a team effort. If you refuse to help with anything, you risk damaging bonds with administrators and/or colleagues. This could also prevent you from receiving support from others when needed.

> "Saying 'no' is difficult, but the guilt associated with saying 'yes' is often worse than the guilt associated with saying 'no'"
> — *Scott Hanselman,*
> *Productivity Expert*
> (Schreiber, 2014, p. 8)

Determine which commitments are reasonable and continue to make them. For example, helping supervise the once-per-year ice cream party during the lunch hour is far easier than teaching an after-school intervention class all year long. High school art teacher Christine Friedrich suggests choosing one thing you are passionate about and volunteering for only that. You might also find that when you say yes to smaller commitments, you have an easier time saying no to more taxing ones.

- **Pull out where you can.** If you are already committed to ongoing tasks, consider whether it's possible to pull out of some. This does not mean going back on your word. Rather, explore whether or not pulling out gracefully is possible.

> "If you do a job too well, you'll get stuck with it."
> — *Anonymous*

For example, Linda Hand planned the school's history camp every year, an exhausting project. When she mentioned she was tired of this responsibility, she discovered three other teachers had been pining for the chance to take over the camp's orchestration. Linda happily handed over the reins, and the interested teachers eagerly tackled the challenge as a team.

At the very least, share your need to cut back. Let administrators and colleagues know when you are feeling overwhelmed, and they will likely look elsewhere when they need volunteers.

Troubleshoot Trends

Having to say no to an onslaught of requests for your time is exhausting. Occasional requests (and commitments) are a reasonable aspect of the teaching profession. When these requests are constant, however, there is often an underlying problem.

The following strategies can help you advocate for changes to minimize your school's demands on teachers' time. Apply these strategies as appropriate for your circumstances:

- **Suggest student volunteers.** A student doesn't have a teacher's expertise, but students can still work wonders. For example, one teacher leading Lunchtime Homework Help (LHH) with five student volunteers trained as peer tutors can be even more effective than two teachers staffing LHH alone. Students can earn recognition and awards for their service, as well as experience for their college applications.

Student: If you need volunteers, you should ask our school crossing guard.

Principal: What makes you think our crossing guard would be a good volunteer?

Student: She's always talking about how she needs to complete 100 hours of community service.

Cameron (2014) describes the effectiveness of a student-run writing center where high school students were selected and trained by their teacher as writing consultants who manned a writing center a few hours per week in a designated room. Consultants, who weren't allowed to write on students' papers, helped their peers brainstorm on topics, question their work, craft thesis statements, and support ideas. This kind of setup, which could also work at other grade levels, frees teachers from providing after-hours writing help, empowers students, and further solidifies the consultants' own writing skills.

If appropriate, suggest your administrator consider student volunteers for a particular teacher-led duty. Even if the suggestion is initially ignored, making this suggestion often can get your administrators considering students for future tasks.

- **Suggest noneducator volunteers.** Consider whether parent or community members would be appropriate volunteers to replace teachers' tasks. If so, suggest this change. If done effectively, parent and community involvement strengthens relationships and helps build a positive network around students.

  For example, teachers at Linda Hand's school oversaw the athletic "Grade vs. Grade Student Olympics" school event each year. When Linda initiated the recruitment of parents to help with this task, the number of teacher volunteers needed was nearly cut in half. Linda merely suggested her administrator share the idea with the PTA and include a recruitment flier on the school's online parent portal, a suggestion that took merely 5 minutes to offer.

  Other examples abound. To combat teacher turnover, Ascend Charter Schools enlisted college students to help middle schoolers with homework and enlisted community members and partner organizations to offer after-school enrichment activities (like karate, African drumming, and dance; Neufeldnov, 2014). YES Prep, one of the highest-performing charter networks, offers students enriching experiences outside of the classroom run by people other than teachers such as through summer camps, international travel, and wilderness trips (Neufeldnov, 2014). It requires very little effort to suggest similar solutions to those asking for your help.

- **Lean in.** Advocating for gender balance in volunteer duties can relieve you of some tasks and—whether you are male or female—allow you to benefit from a more functional workplace. In workplaces, women tend to help more with "office housework" such as helping with the staff holiday party, bringing cupcakes, taking notes, helping a colleague with a presentation, serving on committees and planning meetings, and so on, even though women benefit less from it than their male peers (e.g., being a helper can actually work against a woman's promotion; Sandberg & Grant, 2015).

> "There's no way there would have been a Microsoft without what [my math and drama teachers] did."
>
> — *Bill Gates*

For example, three studies confirmed altruistic citizenship behavior at work is assumed to be less optional for women, enhances the favorability of men's (but not women's) evaluations, and hurts the favorability of women (but not men) when it is withheld (Heilman & Chen, 2005). This added help takes a psychological toll, and 183 different studies worldwide confirm women are significantly more likely to be emotionally exhausted; in fact, for every 100 employees, 8 more women than men burn out (Sandberg & Grant, 2015).

Pay attention to the gender balance among "housework" tasks at your school site. Since most teachers are female, consider the percentage of each gender helping out rather than the number of each gender. For example, if there are just five men at your school and 95 women, men should help with 5% of the "housework" rather than 50%.

Neither gender should bear the bulk of shared responsibilities. "Lean in" by discussing any serious inequities with your administrators. For example, when Lane Rankin, CEO/president of Illuminate Education, recognized gender inequity in office chores, he discussed the matter with the entire staff, and he charged the men with volunteering as often as the women for tasks like taking the notes for meetings and planning office events. He even set an example by announcing he'd clean the staff refrigerator that day (a dreaded task). Lane and his staff noticed an immediate improvement.

Advocating for gender balance in school volunteer or "housework" duties can promote added involvement that can reduce an excess in your own commitment, whether you are male or female. Also, applaud those leaning in around you—both male and female.

- **Point out inefficiencies.** When I was an undergraduate student at UC Santa Barbara, I volunteered for the campus's environmentalist group. I asked where my help was needed and was charged with making phone calls to group members at a makeshift call station 2 hours per week. For my first week, I was supposed to call members to see if they (like me) could volunteer one night per week to make phone calls on behalf of the group. I had little success. For my second week, I discovered I was supposed to use the same script: to merely recruit people to recruit people. That's when I quit and found a different group that could better apply my help. There seemed no point to the phone calls if their only purpose was to perpetuate my volunteer time.

Look for inefficiencies with the volunteer tasks at your school. Sometimes administrators don't see these problems because they are too far removed from them. Your added insight and suggestions can save you and others from unnecessary volunteering or at least reduce the time required.

Reflection Exercises

The following items can be answered individually and/or discussed as a group.

1. Compose a "no" statement you feel comfortable saying when asked to make an optional commitment that would leave you overburdened.

    _____
    _____
    _____
    _____

2. Describe the types of volunteer commitments at your school that would leave you overtaxed versus those to which you could comfortably commit.

    Overtaxing Commitments: Comfortable Commitments:

    _____   _____
    _____   _____
    _____   _____
    _____   _____

3. Think of a typical task for which teachers are asked to volunteer that would also be a suitable task for nonteacher volunteers. Write what you could say to your administrator to propose nonteacher volunteers for the task. Include details on how such an arrangement could work and be a favorable, viable option.

    _____
    _____
    _____
    _____

4. Reflect on your current or most recent workplace. Describe its gender balance or imbalance among workplace housework, as described in this chapter.

    _____
    _____
    _____
    _____

5. Reflect on your curre.nt or most recent workplace. Describe how a current volunteer task could possibly be made more efficient.

    _____
    _____
    _____
    _____

References

Cameron, K. (2014, November 14). 5 ways to take the grind out of grading papers. *Classroom 2.0*. Retrieved from http://www.classroom20.com/forum/topics/5-ways-to-take-the-grind-out-of-grading-papers-1

Heilman, M. E., & Chen, J. J. (2005, May). Same behavior, different consequences: Reactions to men's and women's altruistic citizenship behavior. *Journal of Applied Psychology, 90*(3), 431–441.

Inandi, Y., & Buyukozkan, A. S. (2013). The effect of organizational citizenship behaviours of primary school teachers on their burnout. *Educational Sciences: Theory and Practice, 13*(3), 1545–1550.

Neufeldnov, S. (2014, November 10). Can a teacher be too dedicated? *The Atlantic*. Retrieved from http://m.theatlantic.com/national/archive/2014/11/can-a-teacher-be-too-dedicated/382563/?single_page=true

Sandberg, S., & Grant, A. (2015, February 6). Madam C.E.O., get me a coffee. *The New York Times*. Retrieved from http://www.nytimes.com/2015/02/08/opinion/sunday/sheryl-sandberg-and-adam-grant-on-women-doing-office-housework.html

Schreiber, D. (2014, March 25). How to scale yourself and get more done than you thought possible. *Zapier*. Retrieved from https://zapier.com/blog/scale-yourself-scott-hanselman/

Skovholt, T. M., & Trotter-Mathison, M. J. (2011). *The resilient practitioner: Burnout prevention and self-care strategies for counselors, therapists, teachers, and health professionals* (2nd ed.). New York, NY: Routledge, Taylor and Francis Group, LLC.

Collaboration

8 | "No Offense, but I Prefer to Work Alone"

Teacher Confession: "I really love people. I just never like working with people on projects. Even when they think they've put together a complete, quality lesson, it's full of flaws. Why waste my time fixing a mess and risk offending the teacher who made it when I can just do a good job alone?"

— *Ike N. Dewitt*

Teacher Confession: "I would enjoy working with others if it didn't take so much time. In the time it takes to meet with another teacher, discuss what we're each doing in our classrooms, find common ground, etc. . . . I could have designed an entire lesson myself in that time."

— *M. Payshent*

A lack of community is one of the primary factors that creates burnout at work (Maslach & Leiter, 2008; Skovholt & Trotter-Mathison, 2011). Teachers collaborating and sharing responsibility for all students' success improves teacher retention and satisfaction yet is atypical; for example, a survey of 486 newer K–12 teachers revealed 50% to 66% of teachers plan and teach alone, and fewer than 50% work at schools where teachers concern themselves with students outside their own classrooms (McClure, 2008).

Conversely, the building and maintaining of support networks was found to prevent and alleviate burnout, such as with healthcare workers (Demir et al., 2003; Espeland, 2006; Thomas &

> "Never doubt that a small group of thoughtful, committed citizens can change the world. Indeed, it is the only thing that ever has.
> — *Margaret Mead*

Lankau, 2009). When teachers collaborate, it benefits students and the school, and it also benefits teachers by giving them the support and time needed to handle challenges and succeed (Sparks, 2013).

A survey of 2,000 current and former teachers revealed lower turnover rates when teachers collaborated, as well as greater personal satisfaction and strong collegial relationships (McClure, 2008). Likewise, a national poll of 1,002 full-time teachers revealed that collaboration occurring in schools is one of the top reasons teachers would recommend the profession to others (University of Phoenix, 2015). According to a survey of more than 10,000 teachers, the number-one activity that teachers reported as helping them "learn how to improve the most" was "informal collaboration," and this activity was rated especially high by the survey's top-performing teachers (TNTP, 2015).

This chapter uses lesson planning (and the creation or acquisition of related items) in its examples. However, the strategies can be extended to other collaborative projects, too. For example, teachers can partner with one another through a variety of means to form professional learning networks (PLNs) to help one another grow and flourish.

When it comes to lesson plan collaboration, I relate to Ike N. Dewitt from this chapter's teacher confessions. I shared all my lessons with my colleagues, but using another teacher's lesson plan was hard for me. It took three realizations to topple my resistance:

- Solo planning is too inefficient to sustain long term.
- My focus areas might be another teacher's blind spots, but that teacher's focus areas might be my blind spots.
- Lesson quality improves with multiple teachers' input.

These realizations are covered in the next section ("Prime Your Outlook").

"Be open to collaboration. Other people and other people's ideas are often better than your own. Find a group of people who challenge and inspire you, spend a lot of time with them, and it will change your life."

— Amy Poehler

In this chapter's teacher confessions, M. Payshent's oversight is in not looking beyond a single lesson. Sure, that first collaboration might take frustratingly long to produce. Each subsequent lesson, however, will require increasingly less time and effort. This chapter has a section on how to improve collaboration's odds for success in order to minimize any frustrations.

Prime Your Outlook

If you collaborate while looking for a way out, you will likely benefit less and stop prematurely. The following strategies can help you prepare your mindset for collaboration with colleagues. Apply these strategies as appropriate for your circumstances:

- **Understand solo planning is too inefficient to sustain long term.** Imagine if a five-star restaurant restricted each of its chefs to cooking for a single table of diners, saying, "You take care of your diners and I'll take care of mine." In such a restaurant, chefs would be duplicating each other's tasks, the food would take longer to make, and dishes wouldn't benefit from every chef's specialties. In reality, a five-star kitchen cares about all the diners, with every chef applying his or her skills as needed. That's a large part of why the service is great and the food is delicious.

  Collaborating with colleagues (such as with a partner, group, or department) allows multiple professionals to share the workload, thus reducing each participant's load. Given the overwhelming demands on a teacher (see the "Help Is on the Way" chapter for statistics), it is unreasonable for each teacher to plan in isolation.

- **Understand our focus areas might be another teacher's blind spots, but that teacher's focus areas might be our blind spots.** I knew a teacher—let's call him Justin Tertain—whose primary aims were that lessons be fun for the kids. Students had a blast in their mock sword battles and skits, for example. However, signs indicated the students weren't learning much from an academic standpoint and weren't thinking critically.

  Surely Justin could benefit from co-planning with the department's other teachers. However, Justin also had much to offer. Those same teachers whose lessons were well aligned to learning objectives and focused on rigor used lessons that weren't very engaging. Justin's ability to think outside the box and use unconventional

> **Student A:** Why are those teachers in the principal's office?
>
> **Student B:** I heard them say they were collaborating.
>
> **Student A:** What does *collaborating* mean?
>
> **Student B:** From what I can see, I think it means the same thing as *fighting*.

89

lesson formats could help his colleagues turn their lessons into something more fun and effective.

We teachers have to consider that we might have weaknesses another teacher who likely has other weaknesses can help us negate. Even if another teacher's strengths aren't apparent to us, every teacher has some. Only once we begin collaborating can we find them all.

- **Understand lesson quality improves with multiple teachers' input.** Varied group members usually means varied areas of expertise, and these benefit collaboratively written lesson plans. Plus, other people notice things we miss and have ideas of which we wouldn't have thought. Collaborative efforts improve output simply by being appropriately collaborative. The more you collaborate, the more you will notice this.

Find Appropriate Collaborators

An added obstacle in collaboration is that it takes more than just you to collaborate; you need fellow collaborators. Ideally these colleagues are equally committed to the arrangement and equally prepared to carry their weight.

The following strategies can help you find appropriate collaborators for tasks like lesson planning, assessment creation, co-teaching . . . or any other endeavor you want to co-tackle to help kids. Apply these strategies as appropriate for your circumstances:

- **Consider starting small.** It can often be easier to start lesson co-planning with one trusted colleague rather than a group. Once you and this person have perfected how you work together, you can then bring in additional group members to assimilate and contribute.

For your first collaboration, think carefully about a colleague who is likely to:

- be committed to the collaboration process

- possess good interpersonal skills (e.g., cooperative and considerate)

- be available (e.g., you have the same planning period)

- teach the same subject matter (and possibly similar students, though mainstreamed lessons can be adapted for different student needs)

- follow the same pacing schedule (e.g., you will both focus on teaching integers at the same time and thus will both need lessons on integers at the same time)

Approach your first collaborator choice, and keep trying until you find at least one collaborator with which to begin.

- **Ask administration to recommend collaborators.** A school administrator often has a good sense of which teachers at your school might (a) benefit from a partnership and (b) make good collaborators. For example, Principal Mary Beth Cunat is able to pair teachers not only by subject matter but also by how personal strengths and personalities will complement each other (Thompson, 2015). An administrator's suggestion might even encourage reluctant collaborators to take on the project with gusto.

  Anticipate some administrators might recommend struggling teachers in hopes you can take them under your wing. In that case, make it clear you are trying to stem burning out and that you can only take on an equal partner at this time. Once you and a qualified partner have the collaboration in a smoothly running place, however, you will be in a stronger place to gradually add collaborators who need special handholding.

  District administrators often know about effective groups already collaborating. These administrators could serve as a bridge to establish (and help you be a part of) district-wide planning teams, such as for interested teachers from different schools to join grade level–specific or department-specific groups.

- **Use technology to find collaborators.** You might be surprised by how easy it is to meet educator soul mates through technology. The educator I collaborate with more than any other right now is Dr. Margie Johnson, who lives in Tennessee, whereas I live in California. We met via technology when she read (in EdSurge, www.EdSurge.com) mention of a study I was conducting and reached out to me. Now we collaborate online and present at conferences together throughout the United States and abroad.

  When you share your ideas (such as a vision for lesson planning) with the world through the Internet, you could find someone with your same desire and work ethic. The "Technology" chapter of this book will support you in easy ways to use technology, including social media, which can lead you to suitable collaborators.

- **Get a mentor.** Mentorship's value is often overlooked, but a mentor can actually reduce the mentee's anxiety, cultivate skills, and provide perspective in a way peers and their advice cannot (Perlman, 2013). Adequate mentorship is critical for protecting against burnout, especially for novice practitioners, and an absence of such mentorship directly elevates stress levels (Skovholt & Trotter-Mathison, 2011).

In a national poll of 1,002 full-time teachers, mentorship programs (particularly those supporting first-year teachers) were identified as the second-best way to improve teacher retention, as identified by 53% of teachers (University of Phoenix, 2015). When the U.S. Department of Education's National Center for Education Statistics studied 1,990 first-year public school teachers, 86% of the teachers with mentors (compared to 71% of the teachers without mentors) remained in the profession the follow-up year (Gray & Taie, 2015). Think hard on whether you could benefit from a mentor, even if it's for only some aspects of your job.

Free Resource

EdConnectr (http://edconnectr.connectededucators.org) is a free service that can match you with expert collaborators based on education topic of expertise.

Improve Collaboration's Odds for Success

To reap the rewards of collaboration, such as reduced workload, the endeavor has to go well. Different personalities trying to merge efforts can be tricky, and it takes conscientious steps to ease any bumps in the road.

Lencioni's work on the five dysfunctions of a team can help collaborative teams of teachers be more effective (Sparks, 2013). The first five of the following strategies are designed to overcome Lencioni's (2002) potential dysfunctions, yet all of the following strategies can increase your collaboration's odds for success. Apply these strategies as appropriate for your circumstances:

- **Pay attention to results.** It's easy for collaborative teams to get distracted by conversation and debating the finer points of a lesson. But if your group isn't producing, it's missing its main purpose.

Establishing and discussing the group's purpose from the onset can establish results-driven expectations. In addition, garnering results involves staying focused on output that matters. Lesson planning should begin with an analysis of the standards being taught (e.g., CCSS or NGSS) and a review of the pacing guide (e.g., timeline of when standards are taught). If you stay focused on lessons that lead students to mastery of these standards, with an aim of doing so in a specific amount of time, you're less likely to get distracted by output that is flashy but without merit.

If you don't communicate these points at the group's initial meeting, members can get confused, waste time, contribute less, or withdraw entirely:

- why the group was formed
- each member's relevant knowledge and skills
- what the group is expected to produce
- the work's timeline, and
- standards to be followed (Strathman, 2015).

Once these expectations are in place, pay attention to whether they're being met, and intervene early if they aren't. Other strategies in this section, such as being clear concerning each project and leveraging tools, can make it easy to keep track of expectations and output.

- **Instill accountability.** Tools and clarity, presented as other strategies in this section, can be used to promote accountability. However, enforcing accountability requires speaking up when problems arise.

  For example, if a fellow collaborator regularly misses deadlines and waits until the last minute to honor commitments, address the problem early on. Discuss the added stress this causes all group members, and ask him or her to get better at honoring deadlines. If you do this in a respectful manner such as by confessing your own struggles with procrastination and sharing tips you found helpful, your colleague has a better chance of improving. This will reduce stress for you and others affected by the teacher's procrastination. See the "Keep ahead of schedule" strategy below for more details.

- **Require commitment.** Ideally, you will have selected collaborators who want to contribute and carry their weight in the group. However, problems can still arise. To prevent complications, set and follow clear ground rules. If these rules are broken, see other strategies' tips for intervening early.

- **Set and follow ground rules.** As a group, discuss what norms you want to follow with successful collaboration in mind. Establishing and enforcing these norms clarifies expectations for behavior, as well as time and place (Strathman, 2015). Examples of norms include:
  - Be on time.
  - Keep devices off during meeting time.
  - Demonstrate respect for members.
  - Keep commitments.
  - Speak up and contribute.

Speak up early when the group deviates from its own ground rules.

- **Establish trust.** Trust between group members can be strengthened by demonstrating each group member cares and will contribute. It also hinges on members' ability to behave professionally and treat one another with respect.

  Remember that disagreements are natural in any diverse group and should not be judged as a personal affront (Strathman, 2015). Avoid thinking or expressing assumptions about someone's character, and point out such comments' inappropriateness if you hear them.

  Likewise, keep an eye on how group members treat one another. For example, Ike N. Dewitt tended to roll his eyes when a certain collaborative team member spoke. After being confronted privately about this habit, Ike immediately rectified his behavior. It turned out he hadn't been aware he was rolling his eyes, and he was glad someone had the nerve to point it out to him.

- **Be open to disagreement.** Many collaborative groups fail to benefit from the diverse wisdom available because members avoid disagreement (Strathman, 2015). Discuss the fact that everyone involved should voice their viewpoint, even if it's divergent from that of others. You can still affirm the value of different perspectives while respectfully disagreeing.

- **Be clear concerning each project.** Imagine your discouragement if you and another group member each devoted your time to a particular component in a particular lesson without knowing the other was unnecessarily replicating the same work. Conversely, imagine your panic if you were expecting to receive a finished lesson from a group member one morning, only to find he or she thought *you* were supposed to finish the lesson.

  For every lesson component (e.g., preteach examples, handouts, quiz, etc.) you tackle collaboratively, there should be a clear delineation of who is doing what and when. Tools provide tremendous help with keeping tabs on these tasks and are covered in the next section.

- **Keep ahead of schedule.** The teaching profession is full of surprises and emergencies. Allow for these by setting completion dates (e.g., when you'll finish creating a particular lesson) that are at least 2 days before the lesson is meant to be delivered. That way, if an emergency prevents you from making the deadline, you can avoid the crisis of not having a lesson to deliver. This can also save you from having to do an all-nighter to finish the lesson in time. See the "Instill accountability" strategy (shared earlier) for help keeping co-planners on schedule.

- **Advocate for a schedule conducive to the collaboration.** You need to have planning time, but even more ideal is to share the same planning period as colleagues with whom you're collaborating. You might even garner added planning time if your collaboration endeavor benefits other teachers (such as if you contribute to the CMS for the whole school or district to use). See the "Volume" chapter for help advocating for more or special planning time.

- **Collaborate online when in-person time is scarce.** Though face-to-face collaboration is ideal, a collaboration plan most likely to work with your limitations is better than a plan too ambitious to last. After establishing ground rules and protocols, collaboration can take place online by using technology to share lessons. Though teachers at Wildwood IB World Magnet School meet for in-person collaboration, they also share their work on Google Drive so they can examine and replicate colleagues' efforts even without the meetings (Thompson, 2015).

Leverage Tools

Tools can help you organize, clearly communicate, and track what needs to be done in your collaborative endeavors. An accessible record of these efforts becomes especially important for larger groups but remains important even for pairs.

The following strategies will help you consider and utilize not-too-techie tools to keep your efforts on track. Apply these strategies as appropriate for your circumstances:

- **Consider the use of graphic organizers, calendars, to-do lists, and technology.** Select an approach that works for you and your peers' technology skills, but also develop those skills until everyone reaches a level of comfort with the technology. In addition, be willing to adjust your tool use as the group's needs evolve. For example, you might start out with a simple to-do list on a Google Doc (e.g., just keeping a running tab on what hasn't been done yet, like "Luke and Rush will have Unit 7 quiz done and shared with us in the CMS by Mar. 8"). Then, as your team gets more comfortable with Google Docs and your collaborative process, they can benefit from a chart like the one described in what follows.

- **Use a form to track tasks and their completion.** You can use the eResources chart abbreviated here to keep an ongoing record of what needs to be done, by whom, and when (see eResources for the expanded version, which allows you room to write). This form is meant to have a different page for each school week.

95

Collaborative Lesson Planning Form
(Condensed Version)

 Directions: In each cell, indicate **WHO** is finishing the item or completing the task and **WHEN** it will be completed. Add details (like **WHAT**) as needed.

Details:

Date Taught	Unit(s) ↓	Item:	Item:	Item:	Item:	Item:
Mon.						
Tue.						
Wed.						
Thu.						
Fri.						

Example of a Completed Collaborative
Lesson Planning Form

 In each cell, indicate **WHO** is finishing the item or completing the task and **WHEN** it will be completed. Add details (like **WHAT**) as needed.

Items are considered completed when they are loaded in the district CMS with the access level set to "school-wide" (call District Tech Hotline at 800-000-0000 for help) at least 2 workdays prior to the date taught. The photocopying task is considered completed when photocopies of all lesson components for 40 students are put in each group member's teacher box 1 workday prior to date taught.

Date Taught	Unit(s)	Warm-Up Exercises	Lesson Plan (Activity)	Home-work Assign-ment	Quiz	Photo-copies
Mon. 3/7/16	Unit 7: Author Persp. (ch. 11) & Word Anal. (wkbk ch. 9)	Mark 3/2	Hera 3/2 Clue Game	Hera 3/2	N/A	Mark
Tue. 3/8/16	↓	Alotta 3/3	Kay 3/3 Judge Activity	Jefferson Sch. giving us video project 3/3 (Kay follows up)	N/A	Alotta
Wed. 3/9/16	↓	Mark 3/4	Van 3/4 Coopera-tive Case Build	Van 3/4 Kids Need Posterboard	N/A	Mark
Thu. 3/10/16	↓	Alotta 3/7	Rush 3/7 Writing Activity	Rush 3/7	N/A	Alotta
Fri. 3/11/16	↓	Luke 3/8	Hera 3/8 Story Swap	N/A	Luke & Rush 3/8	Mark

Notice tasks can deviate from lesson planning (e.g., the completed example of this form, above, allows for collaborative photocopying, though this book does have tips on going paperless).

- **Consider using Google Docs.** A Google Doc is a document that can be worked on collaboratively and simultaneously, so that all collaborators can always see the most recent version. Thus Google Doc is a great format in which to chart a collaborative group's efforts.

For example, copy the chart (shown earlier) from eResources in order to paste the chart in a Google Doc to which every group member has editing-enabled access. Members can then visit the doc's link whenever they want to view a task's status or make an update as a task is completed. You all might even agree to highlight pending tasks in yellow and then un-highlight them as they are completed.

> ### *Technology Tools*
>
> See the "Technology" chapter for guidance in how to acquire and use tech-
> nology tools.

Anyone can set up a free Gmail account to use Google Docs. See the "Technology" chapter for details on how to use Google Docs (e.g., how to create and
access a document there). Added considerations for collaborative groups are to:

- Grant all collaborators the right to edit the document.
- Use the chart first with all group members present in the same room and be
  sure everyone understands how to access and use the document.

- **Consider using a CMS.** A CMS is a computerized system, ideally online, where
  educators can create, house, share, and find lesson plans and related components like assignments and assessments. There is often overlap between a CMS
  and a learning management system (LMS). Working on lessons within the same
  CMS will typically foster uniformity on how lessons are written/communicated
  and will make lessons easy to share and access.

  You can typically attach a lesson's related components (e.g., the game board
  that can be photocopied and used when the lesson involves a game, the related
  homework and quiz, etc.) directly to the lesson within a CMS. When the lesson's creator gives all collaborators editing access to the lesson, collaborators
  can typically add these lesson components as they finish them. See the "Technology" chapter for details on using a CMS.

Reflection Exercises

The following items can be answered individually and/or discussed as a group.

1. Describe any reservations you have about collaborating with colleagues.

   _____

   _____

   _____

   _____

2. Explain three ways in which collaboration is necessary for teachers' lesson planning.

   A. _____

   B. _____

   C. _____

3. Identify three colleagues with whom you could collaborate effectively.

   A. _____ B. _____

   C. _____

4. Imagine you and the three people you identified above (in question 3) were planning to collaborate on all of the school year's lesson plans and lesson components. Then answer the following questions (you can get more out of this exercise if you make it an actual plan to collaborate and start by collaborating on the answers you write below):

   What content standards will be followed?

   _____

   _____

   What will be the group's ground rules/norms when meeting and collaborating?

   _____

   _____

   What tools will you use to delineate and track who is doing what and when?

   _____

   _____

   What pattern (e.g., 2 days before teach date) will the completion deadlines follow?

   _____

   _____

References

Demir, A., Ulusoy, M., & Ulusoy, M. F. (2003). Investigation of factors influencing burnout levels in the professional and private lives of nurses. *International Journal of Nursing Studies, 40*(8), 807–827.

Espeland, K. E. (2006). Overcoming burnout: How to revitalize your career. *The Journal of Continuing Education in Nursing, 37*(4), 178–184.

Gray, L., & Taie, S. (2015). *Public school teacher attrition and mobility in the first five years: Results from the first through fifth waves of the 2007–08.* Beginning Teacher Longitudinal Study (NCES 2015–337). U.S. Department of Education. Washington, DC: National Center for Education Statistics. Retrieved from http://nces.ed.gov/pubs2015/2015337.pdf

Lencioni, P. (2002). *The five dysfunctions of a team: A leadership fable.* San Francisco, CA: Jossey-Bass.

Maslach, C., & Leiter, M. P. (2008). Early predictors of job burnout and engagement. *Journal of Applied Psychology, 93*(3), 498–512. doi: 10.1037/0021–9010.93.3.498

McClure, C. T. (2008, September). The benefits of teacher collaboration: Essentials on education data and research analysis. *District Administration.* Retrieved from http://www.districtadministration.com/article/benefits-teacher-collaboration

Perlman, K. (2013, January 30). The often overlooked but invaluable benefits of mentorship. *Forbes.* Retrieved from http://www.forbes.com/sites/johnkotter/2013/01/30/the-often-overlooked-but-invaluable-benefits-of-mentorship/

Skovholt, T. M., & Trotter-Mathison, M. J. (2011). *The resilient practitioner: Burnout prevention and self-care strategies for counselors, therapists, teachers, and health professionals* (2nd ed.). New York, NY: Routledge, Taylor and Francis Group, LLC.

Sparks, D. (2013). Strong teams, strong schools: Teacher-to-teacher collaboration creates synergy that benefits students. *JSD, 34*(2), 28–30. Learning Forward. Retrieved from http://learningforward.org/docs/default-source/jsd-april-2013/sparks342.pdf

Strathman, B. (2015, April). Making team differences work. *Educational Leadership, 72*(7), 60–64. Alexandria, VA: ASCD.

Thomas, C. H., & Lankau, M. J. (2009). Preventing burnout: The effects of LMX and mentoring on socialization, role stress, and burnout. *Human Resource Management, 48*(3), 417–432.

Thompson, M. (2015, August 24). Teacher collaboration: Matching complementary strengths. *Edutopia.* Retrieved from http://www.edutopia.org/practice/teacher-collaboration-matching-complementary-strengths?qt-stw_practice=1#

TNTP. (2015, August 4). *The mirage: Confronting the hard truth about our quest for teacher development.* Retrieved from http://tntp.org/publications/view/evaluation-and-development/the-mirage-confronting-the-truth-about-our-quest-for-teacher-development?utm_source=EdsurgeTeachers&utm_campaign=af0dda9d1b-Instruct+182&utm_medium=email&utm_term=0_3d103d3ffb-af0dda9d1b-292335873

University of Phoenix. (2015, May 4). K–12 teachers rate the ability to affect students, life-long learning opportunities and the variety that exists in the field as top reasons to join the profession, Finds University of Phoenix Survey. *University of Phoenix News.* Retrieved from http://www.phoenix.edu/news/releases/2015/05/top-reasons-to-join-the-education-profession.html

9

Tedium

"My Work Is Monotonous. My Work Is Monotonous."

Teacher Confession: "I've always adored teaching. Even that blood-pumping first year, when I didn't know all of what I was doing and was praying my students wouldn't figure it out. I felt alive, and I could see the impact when I got things right. 31 years later, the job has flipped on me: I know exactly what to do, but the thrill is gone. It's all so predictable. I mean, it's not horrible, but I kind of dread going to work just the same."

— *Rhea Pete*

Despite the maddening pace for which the teaching profession is notorious, Rhea Pete's sentiments are not uncommon. Surprisingly, boredom is one of the top five causes of teacher burnout (Elias, 2015).

Cognitive deprivation and boredom comprise one of the primary hazards for burnout (Skovholt & Trotter-Mathison, 2011). Given the strains of teaching, a teacher is rarely bored. However, with your advanced know-how you might experience a lack of cognitive challenge that can be detrimental.

Important Reminder

When considering any strategies in this book, remember to pick ones best suited to your own circumstances. If your job currently has you feeling highly overwhelmed, for example, you'll want to forgo tips in this chapter that add to your workload.

Often teachers who face monotony are veteran teachers who have perfected their craft. If these teachers pursue routine-breaking strategies, many of which involve helping colleagues and students, they can regain joy for the profession while simultaneously expanding their impact.

If you are one such teacher, your expertise is especially valuable. Fortunately, your road to breaking monotony should be more enjoyable than most of the battles new teachers face.

Fight Routine

Saumell (2014), who has taught for over 25 years, recommends fighting routine as a strategy to avoid burnout. The following strategies can help you break repetition in your professional duties. Apply these strategies as appropriate for your circumstances:

- **Brace yourself for change.** If you have slipped into routine and avoided challenges, it could be because you fear change (like most people). A set of studies indicated people prefer status quo arrangements over new ones, especially if existing options have been in place for long periods of time (Eidelman, Pattershall, & Crandall, 2010).

> **Teacher:** Where is your Halloween costume? I thought you were going to be a superhero, but you're wearing comfy slacks, a bedazzled turtleneck, and sensible shoes.
>
> **Student:** This *is* my superhero costume. It's what my teachers always wear.

Make an honest assessment of how you feel about changing some of the ways in which you work—whether those ways be instructional routines, work habits, technology use, or other topics you spotted when skimming this book's table of contents. Identify which aspects of change you fear the most, and consider those fears throughout the change process to keep them from undermining your efforts.

- **Identify what bores or annoys you.** Reflect on:
    - During which routines do you tune out and just go through the motions?
    - Which routines make you slump and think, "Here we go again"?

These might be during-class routines or outside-class routines. If you can't distinguish the worst culprits, your students can help you ("You never look happy during the journal share"), as can loved ones ("You always complain about grading those journals").

The tasks you identify make wonderful areas to renovate. Replace these routines with ones that excite you by following strategies throughout this book (e.g., elsewhere in this chapter or in other chapters like "Volume," "Curriculum," or "Technology").

- **Start small.** You can acclimate yourself to change and avoid disruption in the classroom by taking baby steps. Find small ways to replace your routines with things just slightly outside your comfort zone. For example:

  - Use a different route when driving to school.

  - Eat your lunch outside and in a new place every day.

  - Sit with different colleagues and students.

  - Greet students at the classroom door as they enter instead of standing at the board.

  - Swap break-time duties with another teacher.

  - Wear something new, etc.

> **Teacher:** To fight monotony I started talking to my students in Dothraki. There is no word for *Behavior Intervention Plan* in Dothraki.

As you get more comfortable with change and hopefully enjoy it, you'll be ready to make more significant alterations in your routine.

- **Change up your instruction.** When you're ready for something bigger, changing the way (or what) you teach holds thrilling potential. Saumell (2014) suggests teaching different age levels or grades, varying materials you use, proposing new projects or changes to superiors, or changing supplementary activities you use in class. Jeanette Dreyer, who has taught varied grade levels and student populations over the past 33 years, says these changes have helped her stay in the profession. Elias (2015) recommends applying creativity such as through differentiated instruction or personalization to feel energized and combat burnout.

These aren't suggestions for teachers who feel overwhelmed by instructional planning and are just holding on by a thread. Rather, this strategy is for teachers whose instruction doesn't excite them anymore.

There are so many instructional endeavors that can involve reimagining much of how you teach kids, with research (to which you can add) behind them. Examples include blended learning, personalized learning, cooperative learning, flipped learning, highly differentiated instruction, response to intervention (RTI), gamification, project-based learning (PBL), maker spaces, greater technology integration, and more. Research such movements and find one that suits you and your classroom. You can start small and build, even combining the best of multiple movements. Your class can even become a sample other teachers can observe to replicate what you've done.

- **Subscribe and read.** If you don't struggle with an overwhelming inbox, subscribing to various education publications such as e-newsletters is a great way to stay abreast of exciting developments in education. You can garner ideas for your own classroom and engage in articles' comment section discussions online.

Many e-newsletters are free and showcase educational experts from around the world. Visit this book's eResources for publications you can subscribe to or join communities that welcome discussion. As you find topics in which you're particularly interested, you can read books on them for added expertise. Saumell (2014) suggests developing professionally to avoid burnout, such as researching, reading, and finding an aspect of teaching to explore.

- **Watch or attend.** There is also great video content online that caters to teachers. For example:
  - PBS LearningMedia, www.pbslearningmedia.org
  - The Smithsonian Science Education Center (SSEC) "Good Thinking!: The Science of Teaching Science" free web series: www.youtube.com (via search)
  - Teaching Channel, www.teachingchannel.org
  - Teach Thought, www.teachthought.com/the-future-of-learning/technology/teaching-youtube-197-digital-channels-learning
  - TED-Ed: Lessons Worth Sharing, http://ed.ted.com

You can also search for particular topics on YouTube (www.youtube.com) or Vimeo (https://vimeo.com). Vimeo contains no adult content and is thus more education friendly (and less likely to be blocked by school districts' Internet firewalls).

"It's never been easier to share your ideas and passions with the world."
— *Peter Diamandis*

There are a number of conferences shared elsewhere in this chapter that you can attend, or go to other conferences in your area. Vendors often offer free workshops, so search the websites for products (e.g., software) you use heavily to learn more about possible events. These learning opportunities allow you to connect with other professionals and learn stimulating content.

- **Find partners in change.** It's hard to be bored when you're in good company. Find colleagues who, like you, are up for something new. Then take on a new routine together. For example, you could power walk during nutrition break, collaborate on a new project, start a lunchtime book club, write an education book or article together, and so forth. Anything that gets you thinking and excited is worthwhile.

- **Mentor.** While mentees are known to benefit from being taken under a mentor's wing, mentors also profit from the arrangement. Benefits to serving as a mentor include recognition, better job performance, and a rewarding experience (Eby, Durleya, Evansa, & Raginsb, 2006).

Consider serving as a casual, informal mentor to a colleague in need of support, or serve in a more official, formal capacity. If interested, speak with your principal, Beginning Teacher Support and Assessment (BTSA) Induction coordinators, or other educational leaders who might know of mentees in need of your guidance. Also, don't discount students as mentees. Many students are in need of adult guidance beyond classroom hours and could benefit from time spent with a teacher before school, during lunch break, or after school.

This strategy is not for everyone, as mentoring requires time that many teachers facing burnout are not in a position to afford. Rather, mentorship is recommended for teachers in a position to give their time—meaning they aren't feeling overwhelmed and their work tasks already run smoothly.

- **Pack your bags.** Traveling teacher Lillie Marshall offers guidance at www. teachingtraveling.com/tag/grants on how teachers can travel the world for free with fellowships and programs. Summer volunteer programs are also an option. For example, you can teach disadvantaged youth in the Congo through Africa New Day (contact esther@africanewday.org). Even if you obtain a sabbatical and plan teaching abroad on your own, a teaching adventure of a lifetime awaits you.

Invite Challenge

Sometimes replacing one routine with another is not enough to break your tedium spell. In these cases, consider a challenge. A national poll of 1,002 full-time teachers revealed the presence of lifelong learning opportunities is the second biggest reason teachers would recommend the profession to others (University of Phoenix, 2015).

Putting healthy, appropriate trials in one's own way is a sign of someone with a growth mindset (see Dweck, 2007). Challenges help us grow as individuals and as teachers, model growth mindset for students, and serve students with enhanced teaching.

The following strategies can help you stretch your mental muscles (and comfort areas) in new ways. Apply these strategies as appropriate for your circumstances:

- **Pick areas in which to grow.** Blended Practice Profile (http://blendedpractice.com) provides a self-assessment tool that can be used to better understand your strengths as well as possible areas for improvement. Take this survey and determine areas in which you want to grow. Approach this improvement with a growth mindset and an adventurous spirit.

> "Be bold. If you're going to make an error, make a doozy."
> — Billie Jean King

Self-reflection can also aid growth. Be honest with yourself about a weak area, and consider asking a loved one to suggest one if you are stumped (then listen with an open heart and mind). For example, you might realize you are too hard a person to please. Delve into learning why, aided by books and/or counseling if possible. Devote energy into growing in this area.

The area you pick can also be interest based. Third-grade teacher Julie Dudridge suggests continuing PD in whatever areas you're passionate about (e.g., the arts, geology, music, etc.) and sharing what you learn with students, who become more interested in learning when teachers are passionate. Successful efforts will benefit your students, loved ones, and you.

- **Take on a new project.** A project can be more than changing instruction or a routine. It might even extend beyond your classroom walls. For example, Mary Jade Haney, profiled in Nieto's (2015) book on teachers who last in the profession, coordinated an international trip for students, collaborated with other teachers to create a student drama team, and spurred student flash-mob performances. You might:

  - Collaborate with your administration on implementing a peer tutoring program or offering a new field trip.

  - Compile your lesson plans and sell them online. Teacher Deanna Jump topped $1,000,000 in sales by selling her classroom materials online at Teachers Pay Teachers (Corcoran, 2012).

Places to Sell Lesson Plans Online

Better Lesson (http://cc.betterlesson.com/home)

Course Hero (www.coursehero.com)

Educents (www.educents.com)

Teacher's Notebook (www.teachersnotebook.com)

Teachers Pay Teachers (www.teacherspayteachers.com)

Teachwise (www.teachwise.com)

TES (www.tes.com)

- Initiate a cross-district teacher articulation for sharing best practices and lesson plans.

- Collaborate with a colleague on creating an edtech app startup (subscribe to EdSurge at www.edsurge.com and Edukwest at www.edukwest.com for inspiration and to keep a pulse on the edtech industry, or look into Udemy's Teacher Tech Initiative at https://info.udemy.com/teachertechinitiative.html, where any K–12 teacher can take a free programming class for $10).

- Write a book and/or education magazine articles sharing your expertise (see the long list of publications in this book's eResources for some likely markets).

- Saumell (2014) further suggest starting a blog. Edublogs (https://edublogs.org) is a free blogging service specifically for teachers. It's easy and fun to use.

The sky really is the limit.

- **Take your expertise on the road.** Carol Bright, who has taught at Buena Park Junior High (BPJH) for 16 years, is known as her school's rigor expert. I learned much from Carol about how to get chronically low-performing students to master advanced concepts and skills. When Carol felt stifled at work, she applied to present at the California Association for the Gifted (CAG) Conference, an event she had long attended and admired. Carol's presentation was a hit at the conference. Teachers from other schools (some within Carol's own district) attended Carol's session and as a result asked her to present to their staff in the future. Carol felt a rush knowing she was appreciated and could now impact even more students than before.

Find a conference that matches your area of expertise and apply to present there. Sometimes conference attendance is free for presenters, allowing you to benefit from other experts' sessions as well.

If the conference takes place during the school day and/or if you are hoping school funds will pay your registration fee, make arrangements through your principal well in advance. The earlier you ask, the better your likelihood of securing your administration's support. Arm yourself with all the details (when, cost, PD benefits, and how they will ultimately serve students, etc.).

Ideal conferences at which to present are those conducted online (see text box), many of which were founded by Steve Hargadon. Online conferences can even suit novice presenters who, despite their rich expertise, might be uncomfortable standing before an audience of peers.

Online Conferences

Global Education Conference (www.globaleducationconference.com)
K–12 Online Conference (http://k12onlineconference.org)
Learning 2.0 Conference (Classroom 2.0; www.classroom20.com/page/2012-learning-2-0-virtual-conference)
The Learning Revolution Project (www.learningrevolution.com)
Library 2.0 Conference (www.library20.com)
OZeLIVE! (Australia's Edtech Conference; http://australianeducators.ning.com)
School Leadership Summit (http://admin20.org/page/summit)

Benefits include:

- The conferences are online, so you can present from your own home or classroom without travel expenses.

- There are a wide number of timeslots from which to choose, often around the clock (due to an international audience), so you can opt to present during an hour when you aren't teaching.

- There is no cost to attend the conference.

- As you present online, attendees will only see your slides (which you make and upload ahead of time using a program like Microsoft PowerPoint). This means you can have your notes or script in front of you the whole time, yet no one will see you referencing them.

- Giving a presentation online (the first time you give it) makes it easier to later give the same presentation to a live audience.

- A conference volunteer is present (online) before and throughout your session, so you can get help with the provided technology or with fielding questions attendees post on the sidebar while you speak.

- The conferences are recorded, so you can share the link with others who want to watch your session anytime in the future.

These conferences reach an international audience and are distinguished events in which to participate.

- **Present to colleagues.** When you are making magic happen within your classroom in your unique way, it's a shame for only your own students to benefit. Whatever your educational specialty, chances are your colleagues could learn something from it.

Talk to your principal about sharing what you're doing with colleagues at your school or at other schools in the district. You could present during staff development time or during an optionally attended PD session, and/or colleagues could visit your classroom to see you in action.

Summarize what you have in mind as one to three sentences and/or a few bullet points. This will help your principal see the presentation's value and understand how it can fit with the school's other PD efforts. If you have already delivered the same presentation internationally (see the previous strategy), it will likely increase your principal's interest.

- **Serve as judge.** Many nonprofit efforts in the education space allow students, educators, or edtech providers to compete for accolades, mentorship, and/or funds. These often rely on judges with teaching expertise. Consider applying to serve on one of these judging panels.

Judging Opportunities

California Student Media Festival (CSMF), Sponsored by PBS SoCAL, CUE, Wells Fargo, and Discovery Education (www.mediafestival.org)
Education Connection'sSkills21 Student Innovation Exposition (http://goo.gl/ftEUN7)
Milken-Penn GSE Education Business Plan Competition, University of Pennsylvania Graduate School of Education (www.gse.upenn.edu)
The Undergraduate Awards (www.undergraduateawards.com/get-involved/judges)

- **Volunteer.** This strategy is not for everyone, considering there is a whole chapter in this book on how to not volunteer. However, schools and their students rely on volunteers. *If* you are in a position to give your time—meaning you aren't feeling overwhelmed and your responsibilities already run smoothly—go for it.

> "Volunteers don't get paid, not because they're worthless, but because they're priceless."
> — *Sherry Anderson*

Consider the types of volunteer opportunities at your school and pick one you might enjoy. There might be districtwide involvement opportunities as well. You can also talk to your educator leaders about your likes, interests, and time available to enlist their help finding a fit.

- **Enter a contest.** Whether you pursue a contest for your students to enter or a contest for only you to enter, contests can generate excitement and rejuvenate lesson units related to the contest topic. To find a contest that interests you:

Teacher Awards and Honors

Fishman Prize (www.tntp.com/fishmanprize)
International Society for Technology in Education (ISTE) Awards (www.iste.org/lead/awards)
Mensa Distinguished Teacher Award (www.mensafoundation.org/what-we-do/awards-and-recognition/distinguished-teacher-award; a Mensan student must apply on your behalf)
Milken Educator Awards (www.milkeneducatorawards.org)
National Education Association (NEA) Foundation Awards for Teaching Excellence (www.neafoundation.org/pages/nea-foundation-awards)
Teacher Appreciation White House Social (www.whitehouse.gov/Social)
Varkey Foundation's Global Teacher Prize, known as the Nobel Prize in Teaching (www.globalteacherprize.com)

- Google "Teacher of the Year Award."
- Visit https://twitter.com, type "Student Contest" or "Teacher Contest" in the search field, and then scroll down to find links that interest you.
- Visit www.edsurge.com/d for challenges, grants, and other edtech-related programs.

Also consider applying for awards listed in the previous page's text box.

- **Apply for a fellowship or program.** Fellowships and PD programs generally provide you with refined mentorship to take your practice to the next level, and they sometimes engage you in new roles like policy development. Consider applying for one of the following:

  - America Achieves Fellowship for Teachers and Principals (http://apply.amer-icaachieves.org)
  - Apple Distinguished Educator (ADE) Program (https://ade.apple.com)
  - Google Teacher Academy (www.google.com/edu/resources/programs/google-teacher-academy)
  - Hope Street Group State Teachers Fellows Program (http://hopestreetgroup.org)
  - Teach Plus Teaching Policy Fellowship (www.teachplus.org/programs/teaching-policy-fellowship)
  - U.S. Department of State, Bureau of Educational and Cultural Affairs and Institute of International Education (IIE) Fulbright Distinguished Awards for Teaching (www.fulbrightteacherexchange.org)
  - U.S. Department of Education Teaching Ambassador Fellowship (www2.ed.gov/programs/teacherfellowship/index.html)

- **Become National Board certified.** Visit http://boardcertifiedteachers.org to explore National Board for Professional Teaching Standards Certification. There is much respect within the teaching profession for this advanced certification. Many states and school districts even increase teachers' salaries when they acquire this certification.

- **Join a community.** Even if you are shy or fear technology, there are some simple ways you can get started. This book's "Collaboration" and "Technology" chapters share ways you can get involved in communities, such as PLCs at your school or online forums and Twitter chats. Educators can benefit from founding or joining a *Lean In* circle (http://leanincircles.org), which can empower and inspire.

When maintained effectively, communities invigorate us and foster our personal and professional growth. A missing sense of community is one of the leading reasons people burn out at work (Maslach & Leiter, 2008; Skovholt & Trotter-Mathison, 2011), and teaching can be an isolating experience if involvement with peers isn't actively pursued.

- **Teach teachers.** There are a number of ways you can teach a class of your peers. Any of these allows you to share expertise with a wider audience and thus impact more students' lives.

If you are interested in teaching a college course, try one of the following:

- Visit the "job" or "career" page of your local university's website to apply for a job within its School of Education or separate teaching program. Most tenured professorships require a Ph.D. or an Ed.D., but there are lecturer positions or other support roles that often don't require a doctorate.

- Visit the "extension" or "continuing education" webpage for your local university. These often offer classes for teachers yet rarely list their job openings within the university's regular website.

- Visit the Higher Education Recruitment Consortium (HERC) website (www.hercjobs.org) and search from positions nationwide. Note you can filter these jobs by location and keywords (e.g., if you only want to teach online).

Teach Online for Money

Pluralsight (www.pluralsight.com)
Skillshare (http://blog.skillshare.com)
Udemy (www.udemy.com)

There are a number of ways you can teach outside the university system. For example, consider teaching for a massive open online course (MOOC) or other platform that allows teachers to earn money teaching classes of their own design. Udemy's top 10 teachers earned an average of $500,000 each, meaning some earned even more (O'Dell, 2013). Within 5 years, teacher Scott Allen earned over $1,800,000 selling lessons on Pluralsight, where teachers' average royalty is $40,000, the top 10 teachers' average is $250,000, and the top five teachers' average is $400,000 (Lacy, 2013).

Reflection Exercises

The following items can be answered individually and/or discussed as a group.

1. Describe how you feel about change. Include relevant examples from your professional or personal life.

_____

_____

_____

_____

2. Identify current tasks in your professional life that bore or annoy you. What alternatives are there to these tasks that would achieve the same results in a more enjoyable manner?

_____

_____

_____

_____

_____

3. List three small ways in which you can introduce variety into your daily routines.

   A. _____

   _____

   B. _____

   C. _____

   _____

4. Pick (✓) one of the following instructional endeavors that you have not yet employed in your classroom but could, then answer the question that follows.

   - blended learning
   - cooperative learning
   - flipped learning
   - gamification
   - global education
   - greater technology integration
   - highly differentiated instruction
   - maker spaces
   - personalized learning

- project-based learning (PBL)
- response to intervention (RTI)
- other: _____

How, specifically, will you employ this instructional endeavor in your classroom so that it helps students learn while simultaneously offering you all an exciting experience?

_____
_____
_____
_____
_____

5. If your inbox is overloaded: List four education-related publications to which you could subscribe if a time comes when you have more time to read. If your inbox is *not* overloaded: Subscribe to four education-related publications and list them below.

    A . _____
    B . _____
    C . _____
    D . _____

6. Find teacher PD content at PBS LearningMedia, Teaching Channel, or TED-Ed. Watch a video there that interests you and describe it below.

_____
_____
_____

7. Who in your life would make a great mentee for you?

_____
_____
_____

8. Pick (✓) one of the following endeavors to do, then explain how you will do it now or (if you are currently overwhelmed) in the future.

- grow in this area: _____
- join a community

- present at a conference
- present to your colleagues
- serve as a judge
- take on a new project
- teach a class to teachers
- volunteer

_____

_____

_____

_____

References

Corcoran, B. (2012, September 27). Deanna Jump's ten tips to make a million bucks. *EdSurge*. Retrieved from https://www.edsurge.com/n/deanna-jump-s-ten-tips-to-make-a-million-bucks

Dweck, C. (2007). *Mindset: The new psychology of success*. New York, NY: Ballantine Books.

Eby, L. T., Durleya, J. R., Evansa, S. C., & Raginsb, B. R. (2006, January). The relationship between short-term mentoring benefits and long-term mentor outcomes. *Journal of Vocational Behavior, 69*(3), 424–444. Amsterdam, Netherlands: Elsevier.

Eidelman, S., Pattershall, J., & Crandall, C. S. (2010, November). Longer is better. *Journal of Experimental Social Psychology, 46*(6), 993–998. Amsterdam, Netherlands: Elsevier. doi: 10.1016/j.jesp.2010.07.008

Elias, M. (2015, March 23). Teacher burnout: What are the warning signs? *Edutopia*. Retrieved from http://www.edutopia.org/blog/teacher-burnout-warning-signs-maurice-elias?utm_content=buffer4b919&utm_medium=social&utm_source=facebook.com&utm_campaign=buffer

Lacy, S. (2013, July 8). Lessons from the first millionaire online teacher. *Pandodaily*. Retrieved from http://pando.com/2013/07/08/lessons-from-the-first-millionaire-online-teacher/

Maslach, C., & Leiter, M. P. (2008). Early predictors of job burnout and engagement. *Journal of Applied Psychology, 93*(3), 498–512. doi: 10.1037/0021–9010.93.3.498

Nieto, S. (2015, March). Still teaching in spite of it all. *Educational Leadership, 72*(6), 54–59. Alexandria, VA: ASCD.

O'Dell, J. (2013, June 18). Udemy: Our top 10 instructors together made $5M. *Venture Beat*. Retrieved from http://venturebeat.com/2013/06/18/udemy-teachers-money/

Saumell, V. (2014, May 30). *Avoiding teacher burnout.* British Council and BBC. Retrieved from https://www.teachingenglish.org.uk/blogs/vickys16/vicky-saumell-avoiding-teacher-burnout?utm_source=facebook-teachingenglish&utm_medium=wallpost&utm_campaign=bc-teachingenglish-facebook

Skovholt, T. M., & Trotter-Mathison, M. J. (2011). *The resilient practitioner: Burnout prevention and self-care strategies for counselors, therapists, teachers, and health professionals* (2nd ed.). New York, NY: Routledge, Taylor and Francis Group, LLC.

University of Phoenix. (2015, May 4). *K–12 teachers rate the ability to affect students, lifelong learning opportunities and the variety that exists in the field as top reasons to join the profession, finds University of Phoenix survey.* Retrieved from http://www.phoenix.edu/news/releases/2015/05/top-reasons-to-join-the-education-profession.html

Tools and Processes Can Be Your Friends

Curriculum

10

"I Create More From Scratch Than Martha Stewart"

Teacher Confession: "Now that we are teaching the CCSS, our district gave us boxes of new books, workbooks, etc. But it is not good teaching to just have students do book exercises or discuss topics with no structure. That kind of teaching bores students and provokes disruptive behavior. I need actual, teachable lessons that engage and challenge kids. Lessons that give kids choice, tie in with assignments and assessment, and have all the components (warm-up examples, graphic organizers, etc.) to make it all come together. And I need this for every school day. If I do not find, make, and put this all together, my class will not succeed. But it is so much work, and I am exhausted."

— *Anita Break*

Anita Break's efforts to supplement the school's established curriculum are not misguided. At this point in time, it's naïve to expect teachers to get all they need from the district's adopted curriculum. Even materials officially deemed "standards aligned" were often written for old or different standards and then aligned after the fact, if they were ever even properly aligned at all. For example, remember the statistics shared earlier in the "Volume" chapter: very few texts and resources assigned to teachers are truly aligned to the content standards they are supposed to cover.

Thus teachers are left to find or write their own materials. Yet time spent doing this can be exhausting:

- According to the U.S. Department of Labor's Bureau of Labor Statistics, public school teachers devote more working time (30%) to classroom preparation than to any other professional duty (even actual teaching in the classroom, which uses only 25% of teachers' time; Krantz-Kent, 2008).

- The UK Labour Force Survey indicated teachers of all levels work more unpaid overtime each week (12 hours more) than any other professionals, including lawyers and health workers (Stanley, 2014).

It's accepted that current curricular needs are not met without added teacher effort. Yet those efforts need not be all consuming or involve creating every lesson component from scratch. There are many ways to alleviate the burden, as shared in this chapter.

Use Colleagues' Lessons

Remember the five-star restaurant analogy from the "Collaboration" chapter. Asking each chef to cook for a single table of diners would be inefficient and redundant and result in unnecessarily huge workloads. The same holds true for education. If thousands of teachers have to teach the same content, they shouldn't all be creating that content from scratch.

The following strategies can help you access and benefit from your peers' hard work. Apply these strategies as appropriate for your circumstances:

- **Develop a lesson-sharing system.** I used to keep all my lesson plans and their components (e.g., homework, handouts, etc.) in content standard–specific binders in the staff lounge cabinets beside the copy machine. Colleagues within my department would use these binders whenever they needed lessons, and they could add their own lessons as long as evidence indicated that the lessons successfully helped students master the standards. The binders grew over time, providing teachers with expanding options and variety.

  We used this process before the advent of the CMS, whereas today you can create a similar sharing system within your district CMS. If a purchased CMS is not provided, you can use a free CMS (suggestions are given later). At the very least, though less ideal than a CMS, you could post PDFs of your lessons on a designated page of your district's online staff portal so all colleagues could access them anytime and from anywhere with Internet access. Even if no portal or website is offered, teachers can still build and share resources for free using Google Docs. Talk to your district's edtech or IT director to best understand the options available to you at your school.

  Whatever system you utilize, talk to your colleagues about instituting a lesson-sharing system. If your district contains multiple schools of teachers, all of whom can access the system and understand your sharing strategy, you can further expand the lessons to which you all have access.

- **Collaborate.** See this book's "Collaboration" chapter for additional help getting lessons from your peers. You can:
  - Go Caesar style (divide and conquer), having each colleague plan an entire lesson alone and then putting the lessons together to form a unit.
  - Split up components for the same lesson (e.g., you write the quiz, another colleague writes the warm-up activities, other colleagues design the bulk of the lesson, etc.); this requires more coordination.
  - Work together on everything.

Whatever your approach, review the "Collaboration" chapter to make it successful. Collaborative efforts are usually better than those performed in isolation.

Work With Administration

There is much you can do on your own to reduce the number of lessons you need to create. However, you can also work with your school and district administrators on ways to reduce your lesson-planning needs.

The following strategies can help you and your administration make arrangements that will provide you with a more complete library of lessons. Apply these strategies as appropriate for your circumstances:

- **Push for better adoptions.** Remember the statistics in the "Volume" chapter concerning few curricular resources being standards aligned (despite publishers' claims). If you and your colleagues find your supposedly standards-aligned materials (e.g., textbooks, software, etc.) are poorly aligned, work with school and district administration to adopt better materials. Even though changing a curriculum series can be stressful, your work will be easier in the long run, as you'll have to find and create fewer supplemental materials.

Added Evaluation Help for Science

The American Association for the Advancement of Science (AAAS) Educators Evaluating the Quality of Instructional Products (EQuIP) Rubric for Science (www.nextgenscience.org/resources) provides criteria by which you can evaluate curriculum's quality and true alignment to NGSS.

- **Communicate training needs.** Teachers are not always given the proper training in utilizing adopted tools. A survey of more than 30,000 teachers by the American Federation of Teachers (AFT) (2015) indicated the adoption of new initiatives without proper PD is the biggest factor contributing to teacher stress. Be sure your administrator knows what kind of help you need with current curriculum and resources.

- **Forge cross-school partnerships.** There is often schoolwide reticence to partner with neighboring schools. Sometimes this is due to school rivalries or to negative assumptions about the schools and their staff. Yet educators are great stores of expertise, and teachers and students benefit when schools partner to pool resources.

  Work with your administrator, department, or grade-level team to reach out to neighboring schools. You can develop a lesson-sharing system (as described earlier) for lesson plans and lesson components organized by the standards they address. If you use the same pacing guides, this system is made easier. If pacing differs, however, you can add lessons throughout the year to have a well-stocked lesson bank by the following year.

  If the other schools are within your district, lesson sharing can be made easier by district tools such as a common CMS. However, you can use free, open-source CMS tools to share lessons with districts outside of your own district. Partnerships with outside-district schools will require added administrator guidance, which might involve some privacy or intellectual property right considerations, but such partnerships are highly viable.

Let Technology Help You

Get a technology coordinator or other tech support to help you, as needed, with the previous section's strategies. If no such expert has been designated, enlist the help of a techie colleague, student (computer science teachers can often loan you a helper), or the district office IT department. The "Technology" chapter can help you secure the help you need.

The following strategies can help you leverage technology to make your lesson planning easier. Apply these strategies as appropriate for your circumstances:

- **Use a quality lesson bank or CMS.** CMSs like Activate Instruction (www.activateinstruction.org) and Gooru (http://goorulearning.org) double as lesson banks in that you can access lessons other teachers house and share within the

CMS. Other technology tools are strictly lesson bank sources, where you can access topic-based lessons for a fee or for free. Consider the OERs listed in this chapter, which offer free lessons.

If you visit EdSurge's Edtech Index for Curriculum Platforms (www.edsurge. com/products/teacher-needs/curriculum-platforms) and for Lesson Planning Tools (www.edsurge.com/products/teacher-needs/lesson-planning), you will see an assortment of available tools. You can even set each index page's filter to "free" to find a cost-free solution. The "Technology" chapter offers further support acquiring and using CMSs and other banks of lessons.

- **Use open educational resources (OERs).** OERs (e.g., free lesson plans, assignments, assessments, etc.) are cost-free resources anyone can reference, use, modify, or redistribute. Lesson banks can be OERs. Finding one to three OERs that work best for you and then using them regularly (so you're not having to constantly navigate through new tools and learn their worth) can reduce lesson preparation time significantly. Edutopia offers a guide to these resources at www.edutopia.org/open-educational-resources-guide, and the U.S. Department of Education offers an OER page at http://tech.ed.gov/open-education.

OERs

These resources offer free and open lessons, with numbers provided by Gomes (2015):
Better Lesson (1,000,000 resources)
http://cc.betterlesson.com/home
gooru (20,000,000 resources)
www.gooru.org
Learning Registry (385,000 resources)
http://learningregistry.org
OER Commons (65,000 resources)
www.oercommons.org
OpenEd (712,000 resources)
www.opened.com
Share My Lesson (312,000 resources)
www.sharemylesson.com

- **Search online.** This tip is tricky, but you can find quality lessons online through something like a Google search. This method works best when you have utilized this chapter's other strategies yet a needed lesson or component still eludes you.

See the Google search tips in this book's eResources to get the most from your lesson searches.

If you find a treasure trove of lessons (e.g., you searched for one thing but found a teacher's webpage with 60 quality lessons), bookmark the webpage so you can easily return later. Your Internet browser's help button should offer instructions for its particular bookmarking process. As you compile a collection of favorite sites, you can search these first when another need arises in the future.

> "Because Google is so popular, it's conceited. Have you tried misspelling something lately? See the tone that it takes? 'Um, did you mean . . . ?'"
>
> — Arj Barker

- **Use lesson planning templates or software.** Lesson-planning tools, which often include CMSs and LMSs, can help you think of all lesson components before a lesson has to be taught. Comprehensive lessons are especially important if you are sharing lessons with other teachers who might not automatically realize which preparation details have been omitted. Common lesson plan details include:

Free Resource

EdConnectr (http://edconnectr.connectededucators.org) has more than 100 experts in lesson planning with whom you can be matched via this free search tool.

- Students taught (e.g., Grade 7), with notes if the lesson includes recommendations to assist specific populations (like English learners)

- Subject area (e.g., Algebra II)

- Content standard(s) covered or assessed (e.g., which specific CCSSs, with each standard's entire verbiage)

- Lesson type (e.g., introductory game) and/or brief description

- Preparation (e.g., how many copies of each item to make prior to the lesson, other supplies and assembling needed before students arrive, how to lay out materials at stations, etc.).

- Lesson introduction (e.g., warm-up exercises, prompts, or demonstrations to ground students in the lesson content)

- Lesson directions (including explicit directions to give students)

- If helpful lesson item pairings are not obvious, they should be made clear (e.g., "This lesson goes with the Stem Cell Diorama Homework Project [CMS ID #87354D]")

If you visit EdSurge's Edtech Index of Lesson Planning Software (www. edsurge.com/products/teacher-needs/lesson-planning), you will see an assortment of available lesson planning tools. You can even set the page's filter to "free" to find a cost-free solution.

Reflection Exercises

The following items can be answered individually and/or discussed as a group.

1. Design a lesson-sharing system that will allow you and your (current or future) colleagues to share lessons with one another. Describe this system below and include specific details like what technology you will use and how you will promote use of the sharing system.

_____

_____

_____

_____

_____

2. In the "Collaboration" chapter's reflection exercise number 4, you designed a collaboration plan for lesson planning with your colleagues who teach the same classes. If you did not already complete that exercise, imagine a collaboration plan likely to work for your (current or future) colleagues and you. Below, write an email to the colleagues involved in which you persuade them to participate. The email should also describe what you'd like to collaborate on and how you propose to collaborate (include specific details like technology used and deadline patterns).

Dear Colleagues, _____

_____

_____

_____

_____

_____
_____
_____
_____
_____
_____
_____

3. Evaluate how well your district-assigned curriculum and resources are aligned to the content standards you are charged with teaching. Describe significant gaps below. It is best if you share your findings with your administration to support a solution (e.g., a new adoption or district-wide efforts to fill any gaps).

_____
_____
_____
_____
_____
_____
_____
_____
_____
_____
_____
_____

4. Find lesson planning software that you can use. Identify the software and its website.

_____
_____

5. Find at least one quality lesson bank you will use and answer the following questions about it.

What is the lesson bank's name and website?

_____

For what types of lessons or lesson components will you use the lesson bank?

_____

What is the name and URL (website) for one specific lesson or lesson component you found there that you plan to use?

_____

References

American Federation of Teachers. (2015). *Quality of worklife survey*. Retrieved from http://www.aft.org/sites/default/files/worklifesurveyresults2015.pdf

Gomes, P. (2015, November 18). A marketplace for teachers to sell, share and shine. *EdSurge*. Retrieved from http://www.edsurge.com/news/2015-11-18-a-marketplace-for-teachers-to-sell-and-shine

Krantz-Kent, R. (2008, March). Teachers' work patterns: When, where, and how much do U.S. teachers work? *Monthly Labor Review*, 52–59. Washington, DC: U.S. Department of Labor, Bureau of Labor Statistics.

Stanley, J. (2014, October 13). How unsustainable workloads are destroying the quality of teaching. *Schools Week*. Retrieved from http://schoolsweek.co.uk/how-unsustainable-workloads-are-destroying-the-quality-of-teaching

Technology

"Using the TV Remote Is as Techie as I Get"

Teacher Confession: "Don't laugh at this, but I am seriously terrified of that iPad [the district gave me]. I sat through the in-service, but it was like the trainer spoke an alien language. Everyone nodded and played with their iPads, but I didn't understand anything. She said, 'click the icon' (what's an icon?), 'scroll down' (is she talking about the Dead Sea?). The only word I knew walking in was 'mouse' but that iPad doesn't even have one. Now we're supposed to use these things for all sorts of new initiatives, but it's like everyone around me is starting from a different place than I . . . They speak that same alien language. I'm a smart, smart man, but these new gadgets make me feel dumber than $%@#!"

— *Noah Gage*

There is rising national understanding that educational technology is essential rather than optional, with 92% of teachers expressing a desire to use more educational technology in the classroom and 89% of teachers agreeing educational technologies improve student outcomes (Staff and Wire Services Report, 2013). In fact, a national poll of 1,002 full-time teachers revealed that technology (with the new opportunities it brings into the classroom) is one of the top reasons teachers would recommend the profession to others (University of Phoenix, 2015).

Yet in a report on research involving focus groups and a national survey of more than 400 teachers, the Bill and Melinda Gates Foundation (2012) found technological capabilities have not benefitted the U.S. education system—particularly where teachers are concerned—as much as they have helped U.S. businesses, communication, and lifestyles. Teachers aren't necessarily taking advantage of the full spectrum technology has to offer and thus aren't likely benefitting in all the areas they can. For example, most teachers never used current technologies in their own

Edtech Definition

Over the centuries, classroom technology has been known to include many things. Some argue even the pencil constituted classroom technology for at least some generations. In this book, the terms *edtech* and *technology* are used to describe computerized or electronic tools that support learning, teaching, or related processes.

educations, which makes it harder for them to become proficient in using an edtech product (Bhaskar, 2013).

> "I've changed my password to 'incorrect'—that way when I forget it, it always reminds me, 'Your password is incorrect.' "
> — *Anonymous*

Of course, technology should never be used just for the sake of technology. Educational technology can be effective in improving the classroom experience only if the technology tools respond to the realities of teacher/student experiences (Bill and Melinda Gates Foundation, 2012). Thus each technology tool should be selected because of its unique ability to solve a particular problem in the classroom, with its user maintaining an unwavering focus on pedagogy. The tech tools profiled in this chapter are appropriate for most teachers' professional duties. First, read strategies for acquiring technology and the help to use it, whether you are a tech novice or advanced user.

Get the Technology You Need

Using technology requires acquiring worthwhile technology that suits your needs (e.g., pedagogical, organizational, etc.). The following strategies can help you acquire needed edtech. Apply these strategies as appropriate for your circumstances:

- **Acquire technology.** Of course, you need access to actual hardware and software. The first step is to determine if technology is available. Too often a district has more than enough hardware to meet a teacher's need, but it is gathering dust somewhere because a teacher was told to use it but didn't want it. Licenses for software downloads often go unused because licenses were purchased based on a use estimate, downloaded once for teachers present at the time, and then forgotten.

Share your tech wants with your administrators and other colleagues, particularly educational leaders, teachers you suspect have unused technology, and the district office's IT department. The better you can artic-

> "You don't have good grammar when you type with your fists."
> — C. F. Payne

ulate what you plan to do with the tech tools and how your use will ultimately benefit students, the more effort people will invest in helping you.

- **Make a case to your administrator(s).** Administrator involvement is necessary if you end up needing a district-funded purchase, changes to infrastructure, or approval to use technology allocated for another's use.

Email to Administrator(s) to Request Technology

Subject: Technology Request
Dear _____,
In my class, I'm faced with a specific problem technology can significantly help me solve:
Problem
[Describe the problem here. Be specific and make sure its nature is pedagogical, organizational, or PD related.]
Technology Needed
[Describe the type(s) of technology you want. Include details such as ideal quantity, timeline, links to sample models, and prices (both individual unit prices and the total cost).]
Rationale
[Describe how the technology directly solves or helps solve the stated problem. Include any relevant counterarguments (foreseeing potential reasons for objection) such as why the existing technology doesn't work with the stated problem.]
I realize technology is a precious commodity in school districts and not always easy to acquire. However, I also know you hold our students' interests as our top priority and thus hope you will support this acquisition.
I look forward to talking more about this possibility. Please let me know a time that will work well for your schedule.
Sincerely,
Me

- **Acquire your own technology.** You can acquire many tech tools without outside funding, many of them free or modestly priced. Visit EdSurge's Edtech Index (www.edsurge.com/products), where you can set each index page's filter to "free" to find cost-free solutions.

  Subscribing to edtech-specific e-newsletters can alert you to new edtech developments as they regularly become available. See the edtech-related e-newsletters shared in the "Tedium" chapter and eResources to subscribe.

- **Consider funding.** If your district will not fund technology you need, there are creative ways to fund it yourself. For example, to acquire innovative technology in Laguna Beach's classrooms, Michael Morrison (2015) leveraged varied sources, including donations from vendors looking for a test site to showcase their products. See the "Environment" chapter for funding resources.

Get the Help You Need

A survey of 600 K–12 teachers revealed 50% of teachers report inadequate support for using technology in the classroom, and 46% report they lack the training needed to use technology successfully to help students (Piehler, 2014). Technology use will only run smoothly if you acquire the support you need to use it—not just with a trainer but also sustainably on your own. The following strategies can help you get the support needed to learn to use technology tools. Apply these strategies as appropriate for your circumstances:

- **Get the help you need no matter what.** Trying to use technology on your own can be convenient, can be self-affirming, and can enhance your technology skills in ways that transfer to other technology you might encounter. However, given your time constraints and the pressure most teachers are under, you don't want to overextend yourself. Know and recognize your own limits and get added help if you suspect you might be in over your head.

- **Use the obvious resources you can find.** District office specialists, school-based specialists, teachers on special assignment, colleague experts, mentors, student tech whizzes (computer science teachers can often recommend student helpers), and the like. If you still need help, talk to your principal and district office about support. Many districts have a tech hotline you can call, and some IT departments will send you one of their own team members. If you thank this person profusely and email a sentence of praise to his or her superiors, he or she will often help you regularly.

- **Request customized training.** Rarely is all of the teacher's tech development accommodated by a single schoolwide training session. Such training can be a helpful component of PD—particularly if all staff will be using the technology and are equally new to its use, making such a session a helpful introduction—but more support will be needed. Traditional training session approaches, such as 3 hours on a workday or 45 minutes after an exhausting day of teaching, aren't working; to truly integrate technology, teachers need access to immediate help wherever they are using technology (O'Hanlon, 2013).

  Just as teachers' instructional styles differ, so do many of their technical needs and so does the support necessary to accommodate those needs. With so many teachers requiring such personalization, it's up to you to speak up about the technology and efforts with which you want help. Encourage administration to arrange for groups to get instruction catered to their needs.

- **If you're up for the challenge, use online tutorials** (found via search) or the particular technology tool's help system to figure out the technology on your own. This can be very self-affirming and help you become a self-sufficient techie. Just keep your pain threshold low so that you call in help before wasting too much time and frustration.

- **Take classes.** Apple and Microsoft stores typically offer a "genius bar" of helpers and free classes for users of their products. Education Week offers a "Free Webinars on Demand"

> ## Good News
>
> Technology skills transfer. When you figure out how to use one technology tool, it's usually faster and easier to figure out the next one. That's exactly how those tech whizzes around you started: right where you might be now (or once were).
>
> If you struggle with technology, keep at it. Though it can be hard, it definitely gets easier as long as you don't quit. Take a break if you need it, but come back to technology by the next day if you had to walk away for frustration's sake.
>
> With a growth mindset like that, no technical glitch can hold you back. Pretty soon you'll be one of the tech whizzes to which other teachers can turn.

> "A computer once beat me at chess, but it was no match for me at kickboxing."
> — *Emo Phillips*

list (www.edweek.org/ew/marketplace/webinars/webinars.html), as do many education organization's websites. Ask your district office to offer classes (based on teacher request) that any teachers in the district can opt to attend.

● **Follow curriculum.** ConnectEd (connectededucators.org) self-guided lessons can help you comfortably master a variety of tech tools. The site offers a free Connected Educator Starter Kit with helpful introductions to varied avenues for professional collaboration and learning.

Improve Technology's Odds for Success

Technology can provide convenience, improved efficiency, and reduced workload. However, you are more likely to reap these benefits if your technology use runs smoothly. The following strategies can help your technology efforts be successful and carry minimal frustration. Apply these strategies as appropriate for your circumstances:

● **Keep your frustration threshold low.** When you are using technology on your own, don't be afraid to call for help, even if someone has just helped you. Using technology with a roomful of students can often be more difficult than the same task seemed when a tech expert was by your side walking you through a process. The "Get the Help You Need" section of this chapter can help you get one-on-one help.

● **Pretest your tech.** A carpenters' adage goes, "Measure twice, cut once." The implication is its vital to be sure of what you're doing before you do it.

Technology use is similar. It's vital that you test all technological components and processes before using them with a class or in a multiple-colleague endeavor. For example, if you plan to let all students scan their tests with new software, try doing this yourself long before students arrive; pretend to be a student scanning his or her test, practice importing the resultant file into your gradebook, and so forth. Failing to pretest tech can frustrate students and cost you precious time.

Use the Right Tools

Technology can revolutionize your classroom and your workload, making you more efficient and effective. The following strategies can help you leverage technology tools in key areas. Apply these strategies as appropriate for your circumstances:

- **Use tools that help you organize.** This involves using an online gradebook, going paperless where appropriate, and using online documents for collaboration and student work. See the "Tech: Tools That Help You Organize" eResource for details. Sample tools described include the EdSurge Product Index, Edmodo, Showbie, Engrade, Microsoft Excel, Google Classroom and the book *50 Things You Can Do With Google Classroom* by Keeler and Miller, Google Docs, Survey, Volunteer Spot, Edmodo, and Nureva Troove.

- **Use tools that help you communicate.** This involves using a student and parent portal, class webpage, and parent messaging service. See the "Tech: Tools That Help You Communicate" eResource for details. Sample tools described include the EdSurge Product Index; portal links like Khan Academy, OpenLectures, and specific videos within YouTube or Vimeo; Webpage tools like Google Sites, Haiku Learning, SchoolRack, and Weebly for Education; Edmodo for Parents app; and Remind.

- **Use webcam grading for assignments and assessments.** With the proper software and setup, students can simply drop their homework or tests in a tray under an $8 webcam or hold them in front of your laptop webcam to instantly get multiple-choice work scored (and you can easily add rubric scores or open-response scores on your own). This setup allows students to instantly see how they performed; lets you instantly see performance for the whole class, each student, student groups, and the like; and can automatically populate your gradebook, student and parent portal, progress reports, data system, and more with the new scores. See the "Tech: Webcam Grading for Assignments and Assessments" eResource for details. Sample tools described include the EdSurge Product Index, Gradecam, Lightning Grader, Illuminate Data & Assessment Management (DnA), and Sharpat Kit.

- **Use online grading for assignments and assessments.** See the "Tech: Online Grading for Assignments and Assessments" eResource for details. Sample tools described include the EdSurge Product Index, Performance Matters, Edmodo, Flubaroo, and Google Forms.

- **Use clickers for informal and formal assessment.** See the "Tech: Clickers for Informal and Formal Assessment" eResource for details. Sample tools described include the EdSurge Product Index and a tutorial by Dr. Russell James III.

- **Use a CMS and lesson banks.** See the "Tech: CMSs and Lesson Banks" eResource for details. Sample tools described include the EdSurge Product Index, Activate Instruction, and Gooru.

"Getting information off the Internet is like taking a drink from a fire hydrant."
— *Mitchell Kapor*

• **Use tools for classroom management.** See the "Tech: Tools for Classroom Management" eResource for details. Sample tools described include the EdSurge Product Index, ClassDojo, LiveSchool, and GoNoodle.

• **Use Twitter in powerful (yet easy) ways.** See the "Tech: Twitter" eResource for details to get started, connect with others, and participate in #chats.

Reflection Exercises

The following items can be answered individually and/or discussed as a group. When it comes to implementing the tools described below, note it is usually best to only implement one new tool at a time. Thus the plans you describe need not be followed simultaneously.

1. In order of who or what you would approach first, list four people and/or resources you can turn to if you need help using technology in your classroom.

_____

_____

_____

2. Research edtools that can help you with organization (this can include lesson preparation, such as a CMS). Select one new tool you plan to use. Describe how this tool will help you with your job, and name your next step for implementation (e.g., securing funding, locating hardware, syncing with other software . . . whatever you need to do to start using this tool).

_____

_____

_____

3. Research edtools that can help you with communication. Select one new tool you plan to use. Describe how this tool will help you with your job, and name your next step for implementation.

_____

_____

_____

4. Research edtools that can help you with grading. Select one new tool you plan to use. Describe how this tool will help you with your job, and name your next step for implementation.

_____

_____

_____

5. Research edtools that can help you with classroom management. Select one new tool you plan to use. Describe how this tool will help you with your job, and name your next step for implementation.

_____

_____

_____

6. If you don't have a Twitter account, create one. Post a tweet of your choice, and write what it said below.

_____

_____

References

Bhaskar, S. (2013, October 11). What it takes to make a hesitant teacher use technology? _EdTechReview_. Retrieved from http://edtechreview.in/news/news/trends-insights/insights/624-how-to-make-a-hesitant-teacher-use-technology

Bill and Melinda Gates Foundation. (2012). _Innovation in education: Technology and effective teaching in the U.S._ Retrieved from https://edsurge.s3.amazonaws.com/public/BMGF_Innovation_In_Education.pdf

Morrison, M. (2015, January 27). An invitation to inspiring learning spaces. _Tech & Learning_. Retrieved from http://www.techlearning.com/contests/0007/an-invitation-to-inspiring-learning-spaces/68985

O'Hanlon, L. H. (2013, March 14). Designing better PD models. _Education Week, 32_(25), 16–17.

Piehler, C. (2014, March 10). Survey finds 50 percent of K–12 teachers get inadequate support for using technology in the classroom. _The Journal_. Retrieved from http://thejournal.com/articles/2014/03/10/digedu-survey-results.aspx

Staff and Wire Services Report. (2013, July 25). Infographic: Teachers and administrators want more classroom technology. _eSchool News_. Retrieved from http://www.eschoolnews.

com/2013/07/25/infographic-teachers-and-administrators-want-moreclassroom-technology

University of Phoenix. (2015, May 4). *K–12 teachers rate the ability to affect students, lifelong learning opportunities and the variety that exists in the field as top reasons to join the profession, finds University of Phoenix survey.* Retrieved from http://www.phoenix.edu/news/releases/2015/05/top-reasons-to-join-the-education-profession.html

Getting Everyone on Your Side

Behavior

12

"I'm Bullied or Disregarded . . . by My Students"

Teacher Confession: "This is painful and embarrassing to admit. My class is like a zoo. Once I told three unruly high school boys to lie on the floor and take a nap since they were acting like preschoolers. It was a shameful moment in my career, and it only amused the class and encouraged more hijinks. I had tried so many strategies and was truly at a loss for anything else to do. I know to be consistent, I know to have positive and negative consequences, and I know not to be too strict or too lenient. But it just isn't working. Nothing I try is working."
— *Sue Keeper*

"Disciplinary issues" was indicated as the number-two daily source of stress by the more than 30,000 teachers surveyed (AFT, 2015). Eighteen percent of teachers had been threatened with physical violence at school within the last year—a number that rose to 27% of special education teachers—and 9% of teachers had been physically assaulted within the last year alone—rising to 18% of special education teachers (AFT, 2015). A national poll of 1,002 full-time teachers revealed students' lack of respect for authority is the third-greatest source of frustration for teachers, as identified by 60% of teachers (University of Phoenix, 2015). Difficult student behavior is one of the top five reasons for teacher burnout, yet this can be avoided when teachers improve classroom management skills (Elias, 2015).

"What I hear when I'm being yelled at is people caring loudly at me."
— *Amy Poehler*

When student behavior is a school-wide problem, it is especially vital teachers also enlist the help of others. The "Administration" and "Community Relations" chapters can help in this way. This chapter will cover aspects teachers can control within their own classrooms.

Classroom management is a multifaceted science with many variables, and what works best for one teacher does not always work for another. However, key guidelines can help you avoid common pitfalls, adopt best practices, and find a management style best suited to you and your students.

Explore Lots of Options

A single book chapter cannot convey the full wealth of tactics that exist for improving student behavior. This chapter captures the meat of those strategies for you, but it would be a disservice to not encourage you to explore this topic further, particularly if you are a new teacher or perceive your classroom as out of control.

The following strategies can help familiarize you with many best practices so you can find those right for you. Apply these strategies as appropriate for your circumstances:

- **Read key books.** The following books can help you master the art of improving student behavior:
  - *Classroom Management Simplified* by Breaux
  - *Beyond Discipline: From Compliance to Community* by Kohn
  - *Yes, You Can!: Advice for Teachers Who Want a Great Start and a Great Finish With Their Students of Color* by Thompson and Thompson (note this book will help you no matter what your classroom's diversity looks like)

- **Use social media for research.** On Twitter (see "Technology" chapter for usage help), search #classroommanagement and #studentbehavior. You will see a list of the latest tweets containing ideas for your consideration and links to up-to-date articles on the topic. Other social media sites (like Pinterest) can be leveraged in the same way. Podcasts and videos (e.g., search www.teachingchannel.org and www.teachertube.com for "classroom management") can help you see and/or hear effective strategies in action. Note this does not mean you should use social media constantly (as the "Overstimulation" chapter cautions, life balance is key).

- **Watch masters in action.** In addition to sharing your classroom management PD needs with your administrators, you can share your desire to visit the classrooms of teachers known for smooth-running classrooms. If you have a planning period when these teachers can be visited (common at the secondary level), this can be easy to arrange. However, options still exist for other circumstances.

For example, your administrator might grant you sub coverage for a day or half day if you present a thorough plan to

- Visit numerous teachers known for good classroom management (students can tell you who these teachers are, often with better accuracy than adults).

- Take notes on the effective strategies you witness.

- Share these notes with other staff (such as at a department or staff meeting) and apply them to your own practice.

Another option is to arrange to co-teach a lesson or unit with another teacher, with all of your students combined, to watch this teacher in action. Other options include planned visits to the library or computer lab at the same time. If these shared visits occur regularly, you can pick up a few more tips each time. Find time to talk with the teachers afterward to hear added insight on why they employed particular strategies with particular students.

> **Q:** If a tree falls in the forest with no one to hear it, does it make a sound?
>
> **A:** Only to a teacher, who also caught it passing a note to a friend and sticking gum under a desk.

- **Relocate planning time.** If you have a planning period when other teachers are teaching, arrange to do your less-thought-intensive tasks while sitting in another teacher's classroom. *Even* if you only pay partial attention, regular exposure to good classroom management can make you aware of effective tricks of the trade. If you don't have this planning time option, find other chances to be around these teachers when they are around students. For example, try to serve the same bus-line duty, eat lunch with a teacher who helps kids in his room, or do your after-school grading while a veteran teacher runs an after-school intervention class for struggling students in the same room. As with all recommendations, consider this one in light of any other struggles you might have (e.g., if your need for peace and quiet outweighs your need to improve student behavior, and if the latter is not causing the former, opt for the peace and quiet).

Be Proactive

A key to keeping problems from escalating is to prevent or redirect behaviors early. The following strategies can help you prevent misbehavior or at least be ready for it if it arises. Apply these strategies as appropriate for your circumstances:

- **Honor and connect with students' backgrounds.** Vanessa Burgos-Kelly and Jennifer Burgos-Carnes, profiled in Nieto's (2015) book on teachers who last in the profession, found they could replace despair with hope—for both themselves and their students—by affirming students' cultural identities. I cannot stress enough how valuable the book *Yes, You Can!: Advice for Teachers Who Want a Great Start and a Great Finish With Their Students of Color*, by Thompson and Thompson, is in helping you connect and work with diverse students. Learning a range of specific ways to engage and empower students of varied backgrounds will transform any classroom.

How Do You Rule?

Like the U.S. Constitution sets the tone for U.S. values, rules in your classroom send a message about a teacher's values. Consider whether your rules treat students as a warden's charge (e.g., sit in your chair, don't talk without being called on, etc.). Such rules tell students they are not true partners in contributing to the learning environment. Also, a list of more than five rules is too hard for students to remember (Wong & Wong, 2009).

I used a single classroom rule which, after being discussed as a class on the first day of school, worked beautifully:

Help the class learn.

If a student engaged in behavior that detracted from his, her, or peers' learning, "Help the class learn!" became a mantra the students' classmates loved to voice. Other teachers find success developing rules with students, involving a cooperative brainstorm and discussion on what will best help all students succeed. In either case, the students become responsible, contributing stakeholders in classroom management, which helps set a powerful tone. Better yet, call your rules "norms" instead of "rules." This suggestion comes from math and science teacher Jean Jolley (2015), who notes students understand "norm" as "normal," such as the normal way we do things.

- **Advocate for students to get the specialized help they need.** Consider whether you spend more time lining students up for school-managed discipline (e.g., detention or suspension) *versus* specialized help (e.g., time with counselors and district psychologists). Most teachers spend more time advocating for discipline, which is less likely to have a positive, lasting impact on students than added professional help. The worst-behaved students are often those with the most problems at home and/or behavioral disorders. School districts often have resources in place to help these students, but channels for lining up this help are not always easy to navigate. Cumbersome referrals can become easy as you become familiar with the process. Talk to school and district administration as necessary to advocate for troubled students to get adequate help from specialists.

> "I know I wouldn't be where I am today without my fourth-grade teacher, Mrs. Duncan."
> — Oprah Winfrey

> "My elementary school teacher . . . was the first adult I ever trusted. She spoke to all of us [in] a tone of respect. And I wasn't accustomed to being spoken to that way. [She] made all the difference [in my life]."
> — Antwone Fisher

- **View students in a positive light.** A study of 376 teachers revealed teachers with custodial student control ideologies (i.e., who tend to view students as nontrusting, irresponsible, and undisciplined) experienced significantly more emotional exhaustion and burnout, as well as reduced personal accomplishment (Bas, 2011). Students know if you like them or not. They know if you believe in them or not. If students know you love them, they will move mountains for you. Show your love and be sure it's sincere.

- **Remember how much students care.** In a survey of 66,314 students, 84% of students said they push themselves to improve academically, and 91% said getting good grades is important to them (Quaglia Institute for Student Aspirations [QISA], 2014). Even if students try to mask it, they care about how they perform in class.

- **Solicit student feedback.** Students love to be listened to (don't we all), and their feedback can help you understand their needs, their preferences, and what works best in your classroom. In addition, listening to your students lets them know they are cared about and positions them as true community members in the classroom. When people feel they are an important part of something, they are less likely to disrupt.

See the "Technology" chapter for details on free survey software. Panorama Education (https://backtoschool.panoramaed.com) also offers a free "Get to Know You" survey you can give students on the first day of class. In a Harvard study surveying 315 ninth graders and their teachers, students who were shown they had things in common with their teachers (based on survey results) immediately started to perform better in class; the difference was especially true of minorities and closed the achievement gap by 60% (Gehlbach et al., 2016).

Fishman Prize math teacher Kelly Zunkiewicz (2014) asks students to write in math autobiographies about their expectations, short- and long-term goals, and what they hope to accomplish. She highlights their own "words of enlightenment" (p. 11) in their autobiographies and posts them on neon sentence strips that line the walls just outside and just inside her classroom door. Students literally walk past their own—and other students'—words of encouragement every day. Student feedback becomes a loud message to other students that peers care and want to try hard in this classroom.

- **Leverage technology.** See the "Technology" chapter for details on tools that assist classroom management.

Promote Growth Mindset

Khan Academy and Stanford University's PERTS co-created this free toolkit and lesson you can use to help students understand and develop growth mindsets:

- https://s3.amazonaws.com/KA-share/Toolkit-photos/FINAL%20 Growth%20Mindset%20Lesson%20Plan%20(April%202015).pdf

- **Talk to your administrators.** When an effective administration knows your struggles, it can pair you with mentor teachers who excel in that area and arrange for personalized PD. This sharing also keeps administration informed about behavior with which teachers have to contend in the classroom and empowers principals to act accordingly. For example, if defiance and threats are commonplace in your school, administrators might need to implement a schoolwide restorative justice program and/or rethink disciplinary procedures.

Manage Behavior Effectively

It's important to be prepared, because once students arrive, you might feel like a soldier who just set foot in a war zone. The following strategies can keep class running peacefully. Apply these strategies as appropriate for your circumstances:

- **Seize students' attention before class even starts**. Many teachers find success greeting students at the door. Once students are inside, things should be set up for students to get straight to work, even before the bell rings. Kids who walk in first can even pass out project journals or otherwise help set up the room (especially helpful if you are transitioning between class periods).

  This straight-to-work policy should be daily so it becomes part of students' automatic routine. However, each day of class needs to simultaneously be fresh and new. Thus there should be signs that tell students *get ready, because learning in here will be engaging and fun*.

  For example, every day in my seventh-and eighth-grade English class we played games I created to engage students in learning and applying concepts. For example, we played a card game I made to construct themes from a story's scenes, or I turned the classroom into a department store and had students navigate informative materials to successfully "buy" and "return" their items. As students entered the room, they saw signs of the game's setup all around us and one of the whiteboards decorated with the game's title.

  This created excitement and urgency for getting things started. Even kids many perceived as "gang bangers" used to knock on my door or peek through my curtains before school, hoping to learn what we'd be "playing" that day. Find ways to send a message that each day will be unique and worthwhile in your classroom.

- **Move.** A teacher sitting at his or her desk while students work is telling students he or she doesn't care about what they are doing and possibly doesn't care about them. Circulating throughout the class puts you face to face with each student and increases your awareness of students' needs, both of which help teacher–student relations. It helps you catch signs of potential behavioral trouble before that trouble rages out of control, and it keeps students better engaged in a lesson, which is more likely to run at a proactive pace with the teacher spurring students along. Also, letting students work on a group-centered activity while you circulate and interact with the kids gives you a bit of a breather to fend off burnout (Kerby, 2014).

- **Regularly acknowledge desired behaviors.** If I move close to student Wanda Chat because she is off task, at the same time I can be telling Ohnt Ask, "You're articulating your hypothesis very well." The majority of your feedback should be positive. It sets a good tone and gives students positive ways to seek your attention. See the "Community Relations" chapter for more ways to offer praise.

- **Forgo short-term wins for long-term gains.** Many teachers use strategies that render immediate results (like snapping at a student to sit down) but overlook the greater harm these strategies have in the long run, as they require teachers to continually struggle for class control (Kohn, 2006). As you select and employ classroom management techniques, pick only those that will help best in the long run.

> "There is no such thing as an attention span. People have infinite attention if you are entertaining them."
>
> — *Jerry Seinfeld*

- **Engage students (and be absolutely positive you are engaging students).** In a survey of 66,314 students, 73% of students say learning can be fun, yet only 44% feel teachers make learning at school exciting, and 43% find school to be boring (QISA, 2014). When students are disengaged, they are far more prone to seek nonacademic ways to entertain themselves. Your students *need* to be talking and interacting in organized ways centered on learning, with some escapes allowed for class introverts. If you lecture for extended periods, visit a class known for engaging lessons and find ways to shift your own approach.

Part of continual engagement is improving efficiency so there are no unnecessary periods of downtime. For example, if students are expected to sit quietly with nothing to do while supplies are passed out, it becomes an opportune time to misbehave. Built in "brain breaks," which can be advantageous to students, are different in that students have an objective to focus on during these breaks.

- **Keep things fresh.** Students often misbehave because they are bored or sense their teacher isn't giving them his or her best. Letting instruction, routines, or curriculum get stale

> "Laughter is an instant vacation."
>
> — *Milton Berle*

contributes to both stances. Examine your practice and find areas that have stagnated then change them up accordingly (see the "Collaboration" and "Curriculum" chapters for support).

Fourth-grade teacher Marie Bammer combats burnout by finding ways to infuse change in the classroom. For example, she plays classical music while students are working, leads kids in a little yoga once per week, comes up with fresh takes on favorite lessons with the use of new technology and project-based learning, tells funny stories, gives "brain breaks" throughout the day, and instills a sense of fun for both her and her students.

Turn Around Tough Situations

Despite your best efforts, some problems will arise. The following strategies can help you turn these tough times around and reduce their negative effects. Apply these strategies as appropriate for your circumstances:

- **Diagnose problems.** Individual student behavior is influenced by:
  - peer behavior and group dynamics
  - what is happening in the student's life outside of class
  - academic frustrations and fears
  - regard for peer opinion
  - need for attention
  - hunger and health
  - temperament, mood, and disorders

  For example, 20% of students live in poverty, with 40% of those students suffering extreme poverty (Nieto, 2015). Issues like hunger and inadequate school supplies impact how students behave in class or whether they listen to an assignment being described.

  Trace escalating misbehavior back to likely influences. That way you can focus on treating the source of the problem. For example, if you win over the leader in group misconduct, the group will often follow.

- **Intervene early.** If you even suspect a student is getting off task, it does no harm to move over to where the student is working. If a student walks in with a scowl, it does no harm to slip the student a note that says, "You seem down. If it's anything you'd like to talk about, I care and am here to help." There are many disruptions you can prevent from ever happening at all. Imagine you're a firefighter, and every spark is worth attention. If a problem seems likely to escalate, be sure the child knows what is acceptable behavior versus what is not acceptable and will be met with a consequence.

- **Utilize a private area.** When a student continues to misbehave after your efforts to intervene early, ask the student to move to a location you name that allows some privacy. For example, this might be a chair beside your desk in the corner of the room, where you can keep an eye on the class but still have a self-contained conversation with the student. If you are moving around the class (as recommended), you can make this request in close proximity to the student rather than calling across the room and attracting attention.

Make this request in an assertive yet loving manner, indicating it's only for a moment so you two can discuss what's going on and help the student. If the student needs cool-down time, give the student the option of continuing to work on his or her class project here or to use a sheet of paper you provide to write anything he or she wants you to know about how his or her day is going, what just transpired in class, or what he or she is feeling.

- **Confront productively.** All interaction with students should be calm and free of sarcasm or negative labeling (e.g., it's damaging to say, "Why are you bad in my class?"). The way I always opened a private conversation with a disruptive student was along these lines:

"You're such a thoughtful, wonderful person. The way you just behaved was so out of character, and I want to understand what's going on, because you know we can't have that kind of disruption—it makes it hard for you and the class to learn. So, what's going on today?"

Even if adjusted for student age and circumstances, a compassionate opening can disarm the student, who is expecting to be chastised. Disciplinary points are still made—that the behavior is disruptive and not permitted—but the approach has a better chance at getting to the root of the problem and engaging the student in cooperating on a solution.

I've had students thank me for discipline I delivered with statements like these:

- "I love you too much to skip this chance for you to learn and grow."

- "I love you too much to not inform your mom, because it will help you overcome this habit, and that will make you happier in the long run."

If you need to assign negative consequences, they should not be more severe than the infraction, they should relate to the infraction if possible (e.g., the student writes a letter of apology to the student he teased), and they should be doled out with love. In other words, help the student understand the consequence is designed to help her make better decisions so she can be successful, and you are doing this because you care about the student.

- **Cater your response to the student's motivation.** Rudolf Dreikurs (1897–1972) produced numerous works and solutions still relevant today. He recommended determining which goal the student had in misbehaving (even asking the student for input on this) and responding accordingly. See Table 12.1 for examples.

- **Never send a student to someone else for discipline.** My first year as a teacher, well-meaning teachers invited me to send misbehaving students to their rooms if I ran into trouble. While this practice seemed to offer immediate relief, its true

Table 12.1 Examples of Catering Teacher Response to Student Motivation

Student Goal	Try Saying	Try Doing
Gaining attention	"Can you help me over here?"	Catch the student on task and give him or her clear attention for it.
Seeking power	"We can't continue when you're doing that. Can you help me come up with a solution?"	Find leadership opportunities for this child.
Pursuing revenge/love	"I'm so glad you're here today."	Encourage some compassionate, confident students to befriend these students, who often feel like outcasts.
Showing inadequacy	"You're trying different strategies, which is a great way to solve the problem."	Praise small successes and make it clear you will never give up on this student.

impact was highly damaging. The minute I sent a student to another teacher, I was sending a loud message to the class that I couldn't handle things myself.

The same goes for sending students to the front office. Teachers who send disruptive students to the front office find they need to do this more and more as the year progresses. Since the practice gets disengaged students out of class, many students look forward to the break, as they sometimes care more about immediate escape from class than they do about school consequences.

Administrators who receive students from the same teacher repeatedly start to take discipline of these students less seriously. Students should only be sent to the office for severe infractions, such as when a fight breaks out in class.

- **Remain calm.** Composure goes hand in hand with remaining in control. Some students will actively *try* to get you upset, and it's vital students learn you won't be baited. If a student tries to involve you in a power struggle, educator author Annette Breaux (2015) suggests calmly saying, "I can see you're upset. We'll talk about it when you calm down" (p. 2). Keeping calm further shows students you are an adult they can trust.

- **Develop a game plan for students who drive you crazy.** Every teacher has these, and it is not unusual for a teacher to dread a particular class period or a new day of school due to one or two particular students. Your professionalism can be your secret weapon in these cases.

Along with the reminder that these are fragile kids, after all, resolve to view these students with the eyes of a researcher. When a student is the object of your researching eye, it is easier to step back and assess the student's actions objectively. You can learn and apply strategies, then judge what seems to work and what does not. If it helps, you can log your findings or apply them to a paper or article you write about your efforts (keeping student identities anonymous). Key is finding a way to get the child out from under your skin and—instead—under a lens through which you can improve the situation.

- **Apologize if you mess up.** No teacher is perfect, and many judgment calls are needed to navigate what students are and aren't doing in the classroom. If you mess up, be sure you apologize promptly to students. This models the same good character you work to instill in students.

> "The best of us must sometimes eat our words."
> — J. K. Rowling

- **Know when to call for help.** If you *ever* feel threatened in class, the front office needs to be involved. Remain calm, try your best to keep students calm, and use your school phone or send a runner to call for backup immediately (i.e., follow any established protocols). If you feel threatened on a regular basis, administration still needs to know. Schools in which violence and intimidation are commonplace need to adopt aggressive, schoolwide measures to change the culture of the school. Though in many areas this is difficult, it has been and can be done. Continue to work with your administration (ideally involving your colleagues as well) until measures are in place to make your school safe for students and staff.

Reflection Exercises

The following items can be answered individually and/or discussed as a group.

1. List three specific resources to which you will turn to expand your knowledge of classroom management techniques.

   A. _____

   _____

   _____

B. _____

_____

C. _____

_____

2. Write your new classroom norms below, or else describe specifically *how* you will go about creating them with students.

_____

_____

_____

_____

3. Describe three ways in which you will formally solicit student feedback and use it to improve the environment or instruction.

A. _____

_____

B. _____

_____

C. _____

_____

4. Describe what you will do to seize and hold students' attention from the very beginning of class.

_____

_____

_____

_____

5. Describe specific ways in which you will ensure your class is highly engaging for students (no "interesting lecture" answers allowed).

_____

_____

_____

_____

6. A student enters class with her head down, ignores you when you say good morning, and slumps into her chair. You are busy getting class started. How do you find a way to reach out to her (e.g., let her know you care) within the first five minutes of class?

_____
_____
_____
_____

7. During class a student shouts, "This is f—ing stupid!" How do you respond?

_____
_____
_____
_____
_____
_____
_____

References

American Federation of Teachers. (2015). *Quality of worklife survey.* Retrieved from http://www.aft.org/sites/default/files/worklifesurveyresults2015.pdf

Bas, G. (2011). Teacher student control ideology and burnout: Their correlation. *Australian Journal of Teacher Education, 36*(4), Article 6.

Breaux, A. (2015). Ten things master teachers do. *ASCD Express, 10*(23), 1–2. Retrieved from http://www.ascd.org/ascd-express/vol10/1023-breaux.aspx?utm_source=ascdexpress&utm_medium=email&utm_campaign=Express-11–08

Elias, M. (2015, March 23). Teacher burnout: What are the warning signs? *Edutopia.* Retrieved from http://www.edutopia.org/blog/teacher-burnout-warning-signs-maurice-elias?utm_content=buffer4b919&utm_medium=social&utm_source=facebook.com&utm_campaign=buffer

Gehlbach, H., Brinkworth, M. E., Hsu, L., King, A., McIntyre, J., & Rogers, T. (2016, February 15). Creating birds of similar feathers: Leveraging similarity to improve teacher-student relationships and academic achievement. *Journal of Educational Psychology, 2/15*, 1–12.

Jolley, J. (2015, August 13). Students advise new teachers: From structure comes freedom. *ASCD Express, 13*, 1–2.

Kerby, M. (2014, June 19). Running dry in the classroom. *Edutopia*. Retrieved from http://www.edutopia.org/discussion/running-dry-classroom

Kohn, A. (2006). *Beyond discipline: From compliance to community*. Alexandria, VA: ASCD.

Nieto, S. (2015, March). Still teaching in spite of it all. *Educational Leadership, 72*(6), 54–59. Alexandria, VA: ASCD.

Quaglia Institute for Student Aspirations. (2014). *My voice national student report 2014*. Retrieved from http://www.qisa.org/dmsView/My_Voice_2013–2014_National_Report_8_25

University of Phoenix. (2015, May 4). *K–12 teachers rate the ability to affect students, lifelong learning opportunities and the variety that exists in the field as top reasons to join the profession, finds University of Phoenix survey*. Retrieved from http://www.phoenix.edu/news/releases/2015/05/top-reasons-to-join-the-education-profession.html

Wong, H. K., & Wong, R. T. (2009). *The first days of school: How to be an effective teacher*. Mountain View, CA: Harry K. Wong Publications.

Zunkiewicz, K. (2014). You had my number. In *Languages for Learning*, 8–13. Fishman Prize. Brooklyn, NY: TNTP.

13

Administration

"My Higher-Ups Push Me Lower-Down"

Teacher Confession: "After years with a quality principal, we were cursed with Dev. She was an incompetent bully, and when I questioned one of her horrible choices she came after me with a vengeance. She even took a minor disagreement I had with a student and blew it up into an attempt to have me fired. Every teacher hated her but was too scared to speak up. The staff finally rose up and Dev resigned upon request, but we are all still rattled to the bone. All the joy was drained from us."

— *Iggy Nord*

Teacher Confession: "New standards. New assessments. More kids in class than ever before. New curriculum. New technology we have to use. New strategies the district is requiring us to implement, even though we tried them 10 years ago when the movement was known by another name. On top of this, our principal assigned us a book to read and discuss weekly. It's too much. There is not enough time for all this, and the demands are crushing me. Like I can physically feel it crushing me."

— *Kent Keypup*

Most administrators I've known have been hardworking, compassionate, and competent. The exceptions to this norm, however, can harm students, demean teachers, and promote teacher burnout. In a study of 532 teachers, those who noted they had problems with administration had higher rates of emotional exhaustion (Korukmu, Feyzioglu, Ozenoglu-kiremit, & Aladag, 2012). Of the 30% of teachers who reported being bullied within the last year, more teachers (58%) identified an administrator as the bully than any other stakeholder (like a coworker, student,

> **A teacher and a lawyer walk into a bar.** The lawyer says, "All I have to do is pass the bar and I get my drink." The teacher says, "Every time I can reach my drink, they raise the bar a little higher."

or parent; AFT, 2015). Instances of bullying were especially high for teachers of LGBTQ, disability, ethnic minority, or religious minority communities.

Other administrators aren't unkind, but their incompetence makes teachers' jobs more difficult and stressful. For example, some administrators left teaching because they couldn't manage the job, and their decision making is impaired by a lack of instructional knowledge. These problems are seen not just in some school principals and assistant principals but also in some district-level administrators.

In some cases, administration has the right intensions but is overtaxing its staff. In describing growing district demands as a primary reason he left the teaching profession, Waldron (2014) noted he couldn't remember a time during his 6-year teaching career that a single thing (e.g., busywork, adjusting to major schedule changes, new tests, new goals, etc.) was taken off his plate. Rather, new demands were regularly being added.

Yet all the superb school and district administrators out there are proof that these positions can be used to nurture students and staff. Handling problems with administrators is a delicate matter, and teachers must select the best course of action for their specific circumstances. Thus read and consider the strategies in this chapter, but only select those best matched to the people and problems you're facing. If you have great administrators, as most teachers do, take a moment to thank them.

Prepare Your Mindset

Chances are your administrator is not evil. He or she might be unlikeable and/or bad at the job, but even bad administrators want to succeed and see the school flourish. The following strategies can help you understand from where your higher-up is coming, which can take the edge off frustrations and help you secure progress. Apply these strategies as appropriate for your circumstances:

- **Think hard about the nature of your administrator.** Administrators' jobs can be far more demanding than many realize. Assumptions that an administrator doesn't care or is working against teachers are often misguided and can have divisive consequences.

Before you conclude your administrator is dumb, a jerk, or inept, consider if instead your administrator:

- is overwhelmed and/or distracted by other issues (e.g., district bureaucracy, other problems on campus, etc.)

- is an expert in areas other than the issue concerning you and can grow in this new area

- is trying to meet your needs but has misunderstood them

Even a poor administrator might meet the above criteria to some degree. Being more generous in how you view your administration can help you tackle problems collaboratively and effectively. Administrators often share teachers' frustrations and welcome teachers' help figuring out solutions (Hess, 2015b).

> "It is an impressively arrogant move to conclude that just because *you* don't like something, it is empirically not good. I don't like Chinese food, but I don't write articles trying to prove it doesn't exist."
> — *Tina Fey* (2011, p. 130)

- **Get in the middle of the road.** Change is hard. Sometimes we're aware that we're resisting something because we fear change, and sometimes we're not. Sometimes our resistance is instead prompted by an administration's extremism. For example, some districts' overtesting has prompted some teachers to be against *all* assessment, including formative feedback that could benefit kids.

> "The meeting of two personalities is like the contact of two chemical substances: if there is any reaction, both are transformed."
> — *Carl Jung*

Spend time reflecting on whether a new implementation or administrator stance has some merit. Usually the reality between two opinions lies somewhere in the middle, and the closer you can get to this point the better. If your administration still turns out to be off base, this critical consideration will at least arm you with a better understanding of both perspectives.

Help Administrators Understand

Your administrator cannot help you if he or she doesn't understand your needs (and the same goes for student needs). A single misunderstanding can foster turmoil and squander efforts. Promoting understanding costs little effort by comparison.

The following strategies can help you get administration in touch with anything it might be missing. Apply these strategies as appropriate for your circumstances:

- **Suggest solutions.** Proposing concrete solutions while assuming sympathy for the administrator's situation can help get an administrator (even a seemingly impossible one) to respond positively (Hess, 2015b). When administrators see issues as too large to tackle, they can opt for inaction (a common reaction). However, when you propose an array of steps that can be enacted, it is easier for administrators to act. Brainstorm possible solutions with colleagues, then put the best ideas into a concise, straightforward list to share with higher-ups.

- **Encourage your administrators to think outside the box.** Educators easily accept the fact that meeting all diverse needs of all students is a daunting challenge. They also agree students and teachers face challenges far different than those faced by schools in the past. So it shouldn't be hard to understand that the ways schools operated in the past do not match today's challenges, and new ways of thinking and operating are required.

  Encourage your administration to research nontraditional solutions to challenges your school faces. New schools, charter schools, and schools in poor areas are especially known for applying new approaches, and your administrators can learn from their successes and failures by reaching out to those with similar student demographics as your own.

- **Share your curricular and programmatic needs with your administrators.** In a study of 532 teachers, those who described their assigned program (e.g., curriculum) as inappropriate experienced greater burnout than those who even partially supported their programs (Koruklu et al., 2012). If your administrators are making decisions that make your ability to teach students

> "To understand a new idea, break an old habit."
>
> — *Jean Toomer*

Out-of-the-Box Ideas

Consider these out-of-the-box ideas shared by Neufeldnov (2014):

- To keep and sustain its teachers, the Knowledge Is Power Program (KIPP, the largest charter chain in the U.S.) offers on-site daycare to teachers working long hours.

- YES Prep, one of the highest-performing charter networks, offers students enriching experiences outside of the classroom such as through summer camps, international travel, and wilderness trips that simultaneously give teachers a break.

- Uncommon Schools offers extensive mentoring and training, gives newer teachers lighter first-year class loads and advises them against running after-school programs, provides 3 weeks of planning time before the school year begins (as opposed to the standard 2 days), and has begun encouraging teachers to work normal hours and maintain work/life balance.

- To be a sustainable organization, YES Prep and North Star College Preparatory Academy High School dismiss classes early once per week for teacher training, and YES Prep has also established hierarchies within teaching and administrative ranks so staff can advance without leaving the profession.

- To combat teacher turnover, the director of Brooklyn Ascend Charter School's elementary campus asked teachers what she could do to make their lives easier and achieved 91% retention; the needs she met included hiring a babysitter to watch teachers' kids during back-to-school night and covering teachers' early classes the morning after a late school event.

- To combat teacher turnover, Ascend Charter Schools reduced the academic day by 45 minutes, enlisted college students to help middle schoolers with homework, and enlisted community members and partner organizations to offer after-school enrichment activities (like karate, African drumming, and dance).

- A growing number of schools ease new teachers into an intense schedule by having them teach one class per day and spend other class periods working with small groups and individual students.

more difficult, they need to know about it. Ask yourself if you and your colleagues have thoroughly communicated your concerns and needs to those at the top. If you haven't, schedule the necessary meetings to do so.

- **Share your PD needs with administrators.** Lack of adequate preparation for dealing with the kinds of learning and behavior problems that teachers face in the classroom contributes to burnout. Whatever your needs, find out if your colleagues share them, then contact your school administrators and/or district administrators (whoever seems to oversee PD at your school). Let administrators know about this need and how training in this area will benefit you, your colleagues, and students.

   Encourage administration to survey teachers before and after PD experiences as a means of understanding what worked, what didn't, and what is still needed. Ask administrators to share survey results with teachers so there is transparency about PD's successes and failures and incentive for teachers to offer thoughtful feedback (Hess, 2015b).

- **Suggest staff surveys precede school-impacting decisions.** Lack of control is one of the primary factors that creates burnout at work (Maslach & Leiter, 2008; Skovholt & Trotter-Mathison, 2011). Yet soliciting staff feedback can empower staff and lead to far better administrative decisions.

   Any administrator can easily survey your entire district or site electronically with free tools like Survey Monkey (www.surveymonkey.com) or Google Forms (www.google.com/forms). Just a few succinct questions can provide a clearer sense of teachers' opinions and needs. For example, Dave Westin was better able to support teachers while principal at Saudi Aramco Schools by surveying teachers every midyear and midspring, asking what was going well for them, what issues did they have, and what PD did they need (ASCD, 2015).

   Ask administrators to share survey results, which creates transparency and supports the position that teachers and administration are working together on a shared goal. For example, assistant superintendent Larkin (2015) cites transparency benefits when Google Forms is used to collect anonymous data that is instantly shared with teachers districtwide.

   Ideally, administration should also discuss matters with staff face to face and should give staff active roles in decision making. Soliciting feedback via survey is an easy first step most administrators are willing to take that can have a big impact.

- **Suggest student surveys.** When schools are run in ways that do not adequately meet students' needs, teachers contend with worse student behavior and greater learning challenges. These factors exacerbate teacher frustration and burnout.

Student feedback is one of the most powerful sources of student data, as educators can use this data to guide new decisions and track the impact of past decisions. Yet administrators too rarely ask students for their opinions. In a survey of 66,314 students, only 47% of students felt they had a voice in the school's decision making (QISA, 2014).

If your school's disconnect with student needs frustrates you, encourage administration to survey its students. Quaglia Institute for Student Aspirations (2014) provides an assortment of questions appropriate to ask students, and these can be adjusted to account for student age.

Use the Power You Have

It can be tempting for an overwhelmed teacher to believe the administration—and only the administration—is the one who needs to act on something, because that would mean there is nothing the teacher needs to do (a welcome verdict for someone already overwhelmed). Yet that stance gives administrators all the power in a situation and prevents teachers from acting in ways that can, in fact, help.

Even when faced with undesirable higher-ups, the following strategies can help you be a catalyst for change. Apply these strategies as appropriate for your circumstances:

- **Push for teacher-powered departments.** There are 70 teacher-powered schools in the United States, where teachers have become the decision makers (see www.teacherpowered.org for details on these schools, the movement, and the national conference; Nazareno, 2015). While whole-school change can be daunting for a teacher fighting burnout, teacher-powered departments or grade levels can be more easily achieved. Consider whether your department or grade level would support such a change, and then follow the online guide (www.teacherpowered.org/guide) to get started.

> "There may be times when we are powerless to prevent injustice, but there must never be a time when we fail to protest."
> — *Elie Wiesel*

- **Don't withdraw.** Teachers can often respond to poor regulations, rules, and routines by retreating to their classrooms and leaving poor administration to sort itself out, whereas teachers can do much to change the decisions that affect them (Hess, 2015a). If you catch yourself grumbling about an administrator's decision, ask yourself whether you've shared your concerns with the administrator. Encourage your colleagues to do the same. A teacher who wishes to remain anonymous said:

"Our principal used to assign us books to read. Two of us finally met with him and suggested he let teachers pick their own books based on interest and on a volunteer basis, then share out as teams or with each pair picking a different chapter. He loved the idea! A considerable number of teachers read books, and the sharing was transformative. We only kicked ourselves for not saying something sooner." If you have "better ideas," your administrator needs to hear them.

- **Join the cause for large-scale change.** A national poll of 1,002 full-time teachers revealed policies developed by those outside the profession comprises the greatest source of frustration for teachers, as identified by 78% of teachers (University of Phoenix, 2015). Whatever top-down policy distresses you the most, there is likely an organization that will welcome your involvement in fighting it. Examples include Defending the Early Years, National Center for Fair & Open Testing (FairTest), and Network for Public Education.

Just be wary of the tone of any organization you join. Some organizations' leaders seem too biased to honor research and opinions that support a healthy compromise. Joining an organization with a volatile stance could sour your outlook and exacerbate burnout.

Other teachers have turned outspoken blog commentary (something you can offer, too) into positions as sought-after experts regarding large-scale change. Audrey Watters of Hack Education (http://hackeducation.com) is an example of this avenue.

- **Don't just assume you're being held back.** It's easy to blame schoolwide problems on poor administration, but teachers spend more time with students and have greater influence on school culture. Even if you have ineffective administrators, or administrators too inundated with student discipline or district bureaucracy to lead in other areas, think creatively about what you have the power to control.

For example, perhaps street gangs have overrun your school and your principal seems to have his or her head in the sand. Keeping administration informed of your actions, you and other concerned teachers could organize a task force to research options, collaborate on solutions, divide responsibilities, and reach out to sources for support. Such sources could include police officials, city officials, youth group leaders, student leaders, community leaders, parents, nonprofits, district staff with a stake in the problem (e.g., campus security, the maintenance department responsible for graffiti cleanup, an after-school intervention coordinator, etc.), educators in your feeder schools, other districts' educators who have triumphed over the same problem, and so on.

There is much you can do with merely your administrators' blessing (or neutrality), and chances are you would generate at least some positive outcomes. Of course, some efforts (like the example provided) can involve a lot of work. To avoid burnout, weigh each endeavor against an honest assessment of what load you can carry, then choose appropriately.

- **Take pride in your successes.** If you do not feel respected by your colleagues or administration, don't let that tarnish the pride you feel in yourself. You are the person who is most aware of what you're doing in the classroom and efforts you're making. Give yourself liberal pats on the back, recognize your value, and try your best not to care if you're undervalued.

> "Great ideas often receive violent opposition from mediocre minds."
>
> — *Albert Einstein*

With that said, it doesn't hurt to share your successes with colleagues and administration. They won't know about the cool things you're doing unless somebody tells them, and others could learn from you.

Communicate Effectively

- **Be clear.** Most administrations honestly believe they are providing the support their specific teachers need, yet they are sometimes misguided. If administrators aren't effectively supporting teachers, it is up to faculty to speak up. For example, teachers can rectify poor PD by being honest and specific with administrators while proposing solutions (Hess, 2015b).

Be sure you and your colleagues are sharing your needs with administrators in ways that leave no room for misunderstanding. When speaking with administrators, it can help to provide a concise, typed list of the three points (concerns, needs, etc.) you most want administration to understand. At the end of the meeting, create (together) a concise list of next steps (with each party getting a copy) so there are no misunderstandings about what will be tried or done next and by whom.

- **Be polite and fair.** Enter into communication with a productive mindset (covered in this chapter's "Prepare Your Mindset" section), and be sure your tone, body

> "When tempted to fight fire with fire, remember that the Fire Department usually uses water."
> — *Anonymous*

language, and words match a cooperative stance. Half the battle is lost if your administration views you as some sort of enemy, yet progress can be accelerated if administrators feel like respected collaborators on an issue.

- **Assert yourself.** An administrator is a leader, and leaders tend to respect leadership qualities. If you speak or act meekly, you risk laying yourself down as a doormat upon which others are prone to walk. Speak up. Stand up. Lean in. Find and keep that backbone.

This is very hard for some people, who feel aggressive when they try being merely assertive. If you are one of these people, resolve to grow in this area. Use whatever tricks work for you. Examples include:

- Strike a power pose (like a superhero) in the bathroom stall before a big meeting. Power posing has been shown to significantly decrease stress during chance taking, increase testosterone and confidence, and increase ability to take chances (Torgovnick, 2012).
- Don't let your voice crawl into that high-pitched, people-pleasing space.
- Have an assertive (not aggressive) friend accompany you at a meeting and emulate the friend's communication style.
- Remember you are fighting for the good of students, and they deserve for you to be strong.
- Remember your students are watching, and you want to model how an adult can be assertive, professional, and effective.
- Remember you are representing the teaching profession and are worthy of respect.

- **Ask *how* you can do something.** Asking *how* you can do something rather than *if* you can do it forces you to explain benefits clearly, shifts the effort into a team endeavor, implies flexibility, and makes it easier for leaders to consent (Hess, 2015b). In education, teachers have an advantage here, as it is harder to argue against something perceived as morally right. For example, "How can we get more parents involved here at school?" "How can we ensure teachers have the time needed to plan quality lessons?"

> "Speak in statements instead of apologetic questions. No one wants to go to a doctor who says, 'I'm going to be your surgeon? I'm here to talk to you about your procedure?'"
> — *Tina Fey* (2011, p. 77)

These kinds of questions warrant solutions that people would want to be associated with rather than against.

When posing your "how" question to administrators, bring in solid facts, statistics, research, and testimonies that show a problem is real and/or a solution is needed. That way you can cut time arguing about *if* something should be done, and devote efforts to determining *how* a solution can happen.

- **Back up your claims.** It can be easy to discount other people's opinions. However, when those opinions are backed by research statistics, by school data, or by an expert's published statement, people are more inclined to consider your argument valid and even to back it. See Table 13.1 for sample statements sent to administrators, each paired with support that could be added for a more compelling start to an argument.

- **Keep trying.** If an administrator doesn't "get it" the first time teachers approach him or her about a problem, teachers need to keep trying to get through to the administrator, just as they would for a confused student (Hess, 2015b). This

Table 13.1 Examples of Backing Up Claims

Instead of only writing this . . .	. . . also write this (see reference list for citation details)
We teachers need a student-free planning period or other form of preparation time built into our schedules.	Even when teachers do an excellent job, without allocated time to think, plan, train, and coordinate, the situation is unsustainable (Herman, 2014). On our staff survey, 96% of teachers ranked "not enough time" as their biggest challenge.
We are concerned teachers—particularly new teachers—are not receiving the support and conditions necessary to keep them working here.	High teacher turnover rates can rob students of stable adult relationships, hurt student achievement, disrupt school culture, and be especially damaging in minority neighborhoods when they erode trust between teachers and students (Neufeldnov, 2014). Extensive research revealed teachers with even two modest initiatives in place, such as working with a supportive mentor or administrator, are more likely to remain in the profession (Riggs, 2013).

(Continued)

163

Table 13.1 (Continued)

Instead of only writing this . . .	. . . also write this (see reference list for citation details)
Our administrators need to make intentional, sufficient efforts to give us teachers a significant role in making decisions that impact the school.	When teachers are told what to do yet have very little input, they are essentially disempowered, disrespected, and more likely to quit (Riggs, 2013). Ninety-one percent of Americans believe teachers should have greater authority when it comes to decision making in schools, and 81% believe teachers are capable of contributing knowledge that can make schools run better (Education Evolving, 2014).
Many staff members feel unappreciated by the administration and fear their successes are not noticed or valued.	While teachers appreciate constructive criticism, they also need praise from principals, such as acknowledgment when teachers surpass requirements or when students or parents report something positive about the teacher (ASCD, 2015). At our leadership meeting, seven out of nine department heads reported teachers in their department say administration doesn't care about them.
Administration-mandated changes to the ways we operate are being made too frequently.	Asking teachers to reinvent their teaching practice every year such as by training them in a new way of teaching contributes to teacher burnout (Herman, 2014). In the last 2 years, our district has trained us in . . .
We are concerned our district is investing money in PD that does not meet teachers' individual needs and is not effective.	According to a survey of more than 10,000 teachers and 500 school leaders, accompanied by an interview of more than 100 teacher development staff, school districts' average per-year, per-teacher spending on PD is $18,000, and the 50 largest school districts average $160,000,000 each in total PD spending per year, yet only 30% of teachers demonstrated substantial improvement, and 20% actually declined (TNTP, 2015).

involves trying different strategies. For example, if talking to your administrator as a grade-level group didn't work, try talking to the administrator one on one.

Consider Outside Help

When you involve a third party in a problem you couldn't resolve with your administrator, you risk bruising egos and teacher–admin relations. However, if you have communicated a problem productively and repeatedly to a higher-up who is unresponsive, and if the issue is worth the battle, it is worth looking elsewhere for help.

The following strategies can help you navigate escalated options when problems cannot be resolved with an administrator. Apply these strategies as appropriate for your circumstances:

- **Speak to your teachers' union representative**. You can request to have this colleague with you at meetings with the administrator. The union rep can inform you of your rights and provide welcome support.

> **Teacher:** After school, my principal expects me to cover detention, my superintendent expects me to read this book, and my students' parents expect me to call them, but I only have time to do one thing.
>
> **Student:** You should do the one thing I do when adults are after me: hide.

Meanwhile, log everything. Make a note of the dates, purpose, and any disparaging statements of any meetings you have with your administrator. These records can help your rep understand the problem and are particularly useful if matters escalate.

- **Involve district administration.** If your impasse is with a principal, your union rep might advise you to involve district administration. When a school administrator is problematic, district staff have often heard complaints from other teachers, too, and can yield change in the administrator's behavior. Continue to involve your union rep as necessary to ensure your job and dignity are kept safe.

- **Consider a new school or district.** Sometimes administrators are blamed for problems that are due more to the district culture or school dynamic. The administrator might even be part of the problem but not all of it.

Saumell (2014) urges teachers unhappy with their schools to try finding a new school or location at which to work. This can help in cases where efforts to improve the environment would take too great a toll on you. Remember, however, that you could land in an equally challenging environment. In addition, beginning at a new school involves its own set of stresses.

Reflection Exercises

The following items can be answered individually and/or discussed as a group.

1. Think hard about your most challenging administrator's nature and describe good things about his or her intentions (even if that approach is imperfect).

   _____

   _____

   _____

   _____

2. Describe four things you can do to help your administrator(s) understand your needs and/or a point you are trying to make. You may opt to make this specific to a struggle you currently have.

   _____

   _____

   _____

   _____

   _____

3. Describe how you can assert yourself when working with an administrator (e.g., by employing options within your power).

   _____

   _____

   _____

   _____

4. Think of a situation in which you feel frustrated with administration. Describe steps that _are_ within your power to ignite change.

   _____

   _____

_____

_____

5. Imagine you are going to write to your administrator about an important, specific need to improve conditions for staff and/or students. Write the key point you will make below, taking care to ask *how* you can do something or solve something and taking care to support your statement by citing facts, statistics, research, and/or testimonies.

_____

_____

_____

_____

_____

_____

References

American Federation of Teachers. (2015). *Quality of worklife survey.* Retrieved from http://www.aft.org/sites/default/files/worklifesurveyresults2015.pdf

ASCD. (2015, April). Tell me about . . . Good ways to communicate with teachers. *Educational Leadership, 72*(7), 93–94. Alexandria, VA: ASCD.

Education Evolving. (2014). *Teacher-powered schools: Generating lasting impact through common sense innovation.* Retrieved from http://www.teacherpowered.org/files/Teacher-Powered-Schools-Whitepaper.pdf

Fey, T. (2011). *Bossypants.* New York, NY: Reagon Arthur Books.

Herman, E. (2014, July 25). Teachers can't be effective without professional working conditions. *Gatsby in LA.* Retrieved from https://gatsbyinla.wordpress.com/2014/07/25/lesson-4-teachers-cant-be-effective-without-professional-working-conditions/

Hess, F. M. (2015a). *The cage-busting teacher.* Cambridge, MA: Harvard Education Press.

Hess, F. M. (2015b, April). Speaking up for better schools. *Education Week, 72*(7), 54–58.

Koruklu, N., Feyzioglu, B., Ozenoglu-kiremit, H., & Aladag, E. (2012). Teachers' burnout levels in terms of some variables. *Educational Sciences: Theory and Practice, 12*(3), 1823–1830.

Larkin, P. (2015, April). Say it with social media. *Educational Leadership, 72*(7), 66–69. Alexandria, VA: ASCD.

Maslach, C., & Leiter, M. P. (2008). Early predictors of job burnout and engagement. *Journal of Applied Psychology, 93*(3), 498–512. doi: 10.1037/0021–9010.93.3.498

Nazareno, L. (2015, April 22). Transforming teaching and learning: 7 steps toward creating a "teacher-powered" school. *Education Week*. Retrieved from http://www.edweek.org/tm/articles/2015/04/22/transforming-teaching-and-learning-7-steps-toward.html?cmp=ENL-TU-NEWS2#

Neufeldnov, S. (2014, November 10). Can a teacher be too dedicated? *The Atlantic*. Retrieved from http://m.theatlantic.com/national/archive/2014/11/can-a-teacher-be-too-dedicated/382563/?single_page=true

Quaglia Institute for Student Aspirations. (2014). *My Voice national student report 2014*. Retrieved from http://www.qisa.org/dmsView/My_Voice_2013–2014_National_Report_8_25

Riggs, L. (2013, October 18). Why do teachers quit? And why do they stay? *The Atlantic*. Retrieved from http://www.theatlantic.com/education/archive/2013/10/why-do-teachers-quit/280699/

Saumell, V. (2014, May 30). *Avoiding teacher burnout*. British Council and BBC. Retrieved from https://www.teachingenglish.org.uk/blogs/vickys16/vicky-saumell-avoiding-teacher-burnout?utm_source=facebook-teachingenglish&utm_medium=wallpost&utm_campaign=bc-teachingenglish-facebook

Skovholt, T. M., & Trotter-Mathison, M. J. (2011). *The resilient practitioner: Burnout prevention and self-care strategies for counselors, therapists, teachers, and health professionals* (2nd ed.). New York, NY: Routledge, Taylor and Francis Group, LLC.

TNTP. (2015, August 4). *The mirage: Confronting the hard truth about our quest for teacher development*. Retrieved from http://tntp.org/publications/view/evaluation-and-development/the-mirage-confronting-the-truth-about-our-quest-for-teacher-development?utm_source=EdsurgeTeachers&utm_campaign=af0dda9d1b-Instruct+182&utm_medium=email&utm_term=0_3d103d3ffb-af0dda9d1b-292335873

Torgovnick, K. (2012, October 1). Some examples of how power posing can actually boost your confidence. *TED Blog*. Retrieved from http://blog.ted.com/10-examples-of-how-power-posing-can-work-to-boost-your-confidence

University of Phoenix. (2015, May 4). *K–12 teachers rate the ability to affect students, lifelong learning opportunities and the variety that exists in the field as top reasons to join the profession, finds University of Phoenix survey*. Retrieved from http://www.phoenix.edu/news/releases/2015/05/top-reasons-to-join-the-education-profession.html

Waldron, J. (2014, June 12). A teacher's tough decision to leave the classroom. *News Leader*. Retrieved from http://www.newsleader.com/story/opinion/columnists/2014/06/07/teachers-tough-decision-leave-classroom/10170567

Community Relations

"When I Ask for Support, All I Get Back Is My Echo"

Teacher Confession: "I work in a high-poverty area where parents just aren't involved. The great ones are working two jobs to put food on the table, and the bad ones are drugged out or just plain negligent. There are also many great parents who don't speak English and would probably love to be involved if we could communicate with one another. I know teachers in other districts who have parents volunteering daily in the classroom. I have to laugh about it, because otherwise I might cry. I would love to have that kind of help."

— Al A. Lone

Teacher Confession: "It's really hard when you give a stressful job all you have to offer, then you open the newspaper and read how schools are failing students. I'm not on the anti-evaluation bandwagon and I don't believe in protecting bad teachers, yet I do yearn for more respect from outsiders looking in. This job is harder than they realize. Sometimes I just stuff my face and watch TV to recover at night, only to wake up to face another difficult day. I wish we got support rather than the clueless kind of criticism."

— Hun Zapportid

"Better than a thousand days of diligent study is one day with a great teacher" (Japanese proverb). "Teaching is the highest form of understanding" (Aristotle). We are surrounded by statements about how teachers are everyday heroes and the greatest hope for humankind's future. Yet sometimes those adages don't mesh with what the media portrays about education or with the lack of willingness from parents and community members to support our schools and teachers.

Some of that disconnect is out of teachers' hands, yet there are many ways in which teachers can improve public perception of the profession. Likewise, there are many ways in which teachers can give parents, community members, and other stakeholders a clearer picture of how teachers like you work magic in the classroom . . . and teachers can increase stakeholders' classroom involvement in the process.

Statistics on Parent Involvement

According to the U.S. Department of Education, parental engagement is a key factor in teacher retention, and teachers experience greater satisfaction when parental involvement grows (Riggs, 2013). Sadly, a survey of 1,000 K–12 teachers indicated 97% of teachers want parents involved, such as within the classroom, yet 76% of teachers report less than half of their students' parents are involved in this way, and 47% of teachers regarded low parent involvement as a source of frustration (more so than discipline issues and large class sizes; Reid, 2014). This 97% of teachers included 95% of high school teachers, and 56% of the K–12 teachers indicated fewer than 25% of parents are actually involved in their classrooms (University of Phoenix, 2015). There's thus a disconnect between what teachers need and what they are getting from parents.

There is often a disconnect between what students need and what they are getting from their parents academically as well. For example, 87% of parents believe their child's academic success is based primarily on the child's natural abilities *regardless* of the parent's help (NBC News Education Nation, 2015). As teachers know, parental expectations and support of academics are paramount.

Fortunately, there is much teachers can do to bridge the divide. According to the U.S. Department of Labor's Bureau of Labor Statistics, public school teachers devote only 3% of their working time to parent interaction; no other professional duty requires less of their time (Krantz-Kent, 2008). Yet in a study of 803 American parents (including guardians and primary caregivers) of kids aged 3 to 18, 47% of parents wished they could be more involved in their child's education, and this percentage is higher for low-income parents, less-educated parents, working parents, and minority parents (NBC News Education Nation, 2015). Specific shifts in teachers' efforts can capitalize on stakeholders' desire to be more involved and can render big improvements in parent and community connections.

Maximize Back-to-School Night and Open House

When you stand before your students' guardians, you are like a salesperson getting few chances at delivering a high-stakes sales pitch. You need to win parents' cooperation, encourage their involvement, and secure classroom volunteers.

The following strategies can help you make the most of parent-friendly events. Apply these strategies as appropriate for your circumstances:

- **Exude care.** Parents are most concerned with whether you care about their children, and caring to give students the best instruction is merely an extension of this. "Parents want love, not credentials, routines, and marble jars," writes third-grade teacher Gaetan Pappalardo (2011, p. 1). When talking about the nuts and bolts of how your class runs, sprinkle loving phrases liberally, such as, "I care so much," "Like you, I want what is best for your children," and "I care not just about how your child does in this class but about his or her whole life." Let everything else you talk about and do reflect this care.

- **Improve your parent handout.** Give parents a handout even if your information is all online. Though it may offer a web link to more details (like syllabus content), limit your handout to one post-friendly page.

  Parents have a range of education levels and first languages. Your handout should thus be as simple and jargon-free as your student handouts. Even in affluent communities, your parents are busy and need information simplified. Also, see tips elsewhere in this chapter about translating documents into parents' home languages.

Handouts Should Keep Things Simple

A parent handout might merely cover how parents can best:

- know what homework is due and when (such as through a teacher website like www.haikulearning.com), including test study
- view student progress (such as through a district's online parent portal)
- reach you

- help students at home
- get their students additional help when needed
- get involved in the classroom (make this especially clear at the secondary level, when parents sometimes assume their help isn't wanted)

Also do something to visually make your handout stand out, like putting it on a light paper color or adding a memorable image. This will help parents find the handout among the mess of school papers they acquire.

- **Articulate respect for attendees and their expertise.** Attendees will include legal guardians, but other stakeholders like grandparents, aunts, and uncles are often in attendance (sometimes in place of parents). Many stakeholders have negative memories of their childhood teachers, and it can take proactive steps to prevent stakeholders from extending this association to you or from sharing negative school attitudes with their children. Make it clear you respect the love and guidance they give your students and that you respect their knowledge of students' needs. Explain this is yet another reason the important people in students' lives are a vital asset as classroom volunteers.

- **. . . and then snag volunteers.** Parents who feel welcomed and involved are more likely to cooperate with teachers. Give every attendee a flyer covering varied ways in which a stakeholder can get involved. Make the bottom of the page a tear-off form (so the attendee can keep volunteer descriptions on the top portion) to be dropped in a designated spot before leaving your classroom, indicating via check-box how he or she will volunteer. Put a link on this sheet that can be used by parents who prefer to sign up later.

- **Find other ways to bring parents into the classroom.** Before stakeholders leave your classroom, have them each complete and sign three slips of paper in any language they choose (provide prompts in parents' native languages):

  - Dear *[Student Name]*, I want you to try hard in this class because . . .

  - Dear *[Student Name]*, I know you can succeed in this class because . . .

  - Dear *[Student Name]*, I know you can succeed in life because . . .

Keep these completed forms and share them with students as you see fit throughout the school year. Getting one of these notes at a critical moment (like when a student is frustrated or reducing effort) can be pivotal.

Maximize Parent–Teacher Conferences

Evidence from multiple studies has shown family involvement improves student achievement, school readiness, and social skills (Harvard Family Research Project, 2010). The one-on-one time with parents, sometimes two-on-one when the student attends, is a great time to boost involvement.

The following strategies can help you make the most of times when you meet with parents to discuss their child. Apply these strategies as appropriate for your circumstances:

- **Repeat the strategies above.** Each strategy provided above for the "Maximize Back-to-School Night and Open House" section can help at conferences, too.

- **Publicize.** The Harvard Family Research Project (2010) recommends inviting and reminding parents to attend conferences and provides a tip sheet at www.hfrp. org/var/hfrp/storage/fckeditor/File/Parent-Teacher-ConferenceTipSheet-100610. pdf with ways both teachers and parents can publicize the event.

Conference Resources

TeacherVision offers free, print-friendly parent-teacher conference resources such as letters, forms, sign-in sheets, signs, and more:

- www.teachervision.com/teacher-parent-conferences/resource/3713.html

- **Use technology.** Nowadays we tell parents to view student reports online via parent portals, stay abreast of assignments via teacher websites, and the like. However, these online activities are far more likely to happen when parents are helped through the steps. Have a laptop handy so you can walk the parent through these steps, literally having the parent doing the clicking, unless frustration ensues. Give each parent a *very simple* handout (possibly from a tech coordinator) on how any technical steps can be achieved at home. These steps will increase parents' likelihood of helping students academically.

Technology can also give you face-to-face time with hard-to-meet parents. Often the parents we need to meet with most (e.g., of struggling students) are the ones least likely to meet with a teacher. Yet face-to-face time is the best way to build rapport (Larkin, 2015). If a parent has Internet access and is open to a video chat, you can make arrangements to converse via Skype (www.skype.com) or Google hangouts (www.google.com/hangouts). Be sure the parent knows how to use the tool, and provide him or her with the link to directions for support.

- **Use data.** Sixty-six percent of parents believe their children's overall academic performance and grades are either very good or excellent (NBC News Education Nation, 2015). When this belief is misguided, data use becomes even more important.

The data that add up to a class grade are often perceived as objective, even when scores were subjectively determined. Showing parents straightforward reports from a district data system or your online gradebook can increase parent acceptance of scores and allow you to talk about solving problems (rather than arguing if they exist). For example, high school teacher Nicole Sledge (2016) finds sharing behavior logs with parents allows them to recognize patterns and offers a way to discuss solutions.

- **Show student work.** Grades and other data are easier for parents to accept when they see samples of the work behind it. Bring a folder of each student's work to show parents, as well as anchor papers and rubrics so parents can see how this work aligns with expectations.

- **Provide a personalized take-away.** Each parent should walk away with a clear indication of the child's strengths and weaknesses in terms of academics, behavior, effort, and attendance. A student report from your district's data system can help in this regard. However, parents will also need something uncommon in data systems: a clear indication of how the parent can help with identified weaknesses.

If you put effort into making a *simple* account of how parents can help each child, your instructional burden can be lightened as parents share the load. Keep this list to no more than three things the parent can do; otherwise, it can be too overwhelming and thus not followed. Anytime you suggest parents do something (e.g., "use the district's Tutor Helper"), include easy steps for achieving it (e.g., "visit www.Tutor Helper.com, then click . . .").

- **Limit your concerns.** Just as your list of ways parents should help should be limited, so should your concerns. Former elementary school teacher and PD specialist Margaret Wilson (2011) suggests acknowledging you plan to help the student with several areas but that you'd like to focus on just one or two for the moment. Otherwise parents can feel hopeless.

- **Frontload a negative report with positives.** A student who misbehaves or struggles in your class often has a history of struggles. It is a blessing this student's parent has shown up to hear a report he or she likely anticipates will be negative. Begin the conference with sincere praise regarding the student's assets. High school English teacher Nicholas Provenzano (2014) recommends sharing two positives before every one negative. This will help prevent the parent—or student, who might be present—from feeling overwhelmed or defensive. For example, you might say, "Missy B. Haven has a magnetic personality students love—and I love it, too. I can see her being a leader, entertainer, or boss. To get there, she'll need to control how she uses that personality. We need her to practice this control in class by recognizing when is an OK time to joke around and when is not . . ."

- **Find the best approach.** There is a body of research concerning untraditional approaches to parent–teacher conferences, such as student-led conferences. Use your PLN (see the "Collaboration" chapter) to explore new options and find the one that works best for you and your students.

Get Adults Involved in Your Classroom

When parents and other community members see what goes on in your classroom, it enhances their respect for you and the hard job you do. Plus, volunteers can make your job easier.

According to a 1,000-participant survey by WeAreTeachers and Volunteer Spot (2013), 99% of parents and 97% of educators believe volunteers are good or necessary in the classroom, and 85% of parents and 87% of educators believe volunteering offers parents a chance to support and encourage their kids. Let that sink in: 99% of your students' parents believe you should be asking them to volunteer in your classroom! More than 40% of parents even report they want to volunteer more (Bantuveris, 2013). Other community members, often with more time to spare, can also help.

> **Student to Student:** Yo mama helps out in your classroom so much, you think you're homeschooled.

The following strategies can help you acquire volunteers—parents and otherwise—for your classroom. Apply these strategies as appropriate for your circumstances:

- **Make signup easy and accessible.** As a parent I have seen a long list of volunteer opportunities on a single clipboard at Back-to-School Night that I never saw again. While some parents signed up that night in the classroom, I didn't have time to wait in the long signup line, and I wanted time to consult my calendar while considering opportunities.

Give parents regular access to sign up for volunteering. For example, you can create a sign-up survey for free using Google Forms (see the "Technology" chapter for details). This will automatically track sign-ups for you in an Excel spreadsheet, and you can adjust the form as your needs change so parents are always given options to offer what you need most. You can email the survey link to parents regularly and also print it on any hard copies of volunteer opportunities so parents have the option of signing up online.

Also consider using Volunteer Spot (www.volunteerspot.com), a free online scheduling tool. In addition to streamlining signups, Volunteer Spot sends parents automated reminders, reducing missed shifts (Bantuveris, 2013).

- **Be clear about what each commitment entails.** It is not enough to say, "Help in the class garden" as an item on the sign-up list. Parents need to know what that task entails, if there are certain hours they must be present, if they have to have gardening expertise, and so on. Provide succinct descriptions of volunteer tasks. For items needed, this description should include the price of the item and where (e.g., the web address or store name) parents can buy it.

- **Follow protocol.** Learn how your school or district requires volunteering to be handled (should volunteers check in with the office receptionist? may nonguardians volunteer? etc.). Follow the rules and guide your volunteers in doing the same.

- **Seize unconventional hours.** Seventy-three percent of parents don't volunteer regularly because of their job hours (WeAreTeachers & Volunteer Spot, 2013). Many stakeholders work during the week, so include volunteer options that can be done after hours. For example, these parents can gather/deliver materials for the class, perform tasks at home (like assembling booklets), gather community supporters or donations for an event, or invite classmates over to benefit from homework help they offer their own children.

  Volunteer Spot founder Karen Bantuveris (2013) suggests starting the day with volunteer shifts like reading circles so parents can assist before work, working in the school garden on weekends, or having parents read to the class or help students via Skype or Google Hangouts so they can be present without being physically present. Other parents can't volunteer 1 hour per week but are happy to work a single 8-hour shift every other month, thus offering you the same number of hours but on a day they can take off from work.

- **Vary opportunities.** A single way to volunteer—like running a computer center—will not work for all parents' comfort levels and preferences. Think outside the box and offer a variety of ways parents can help. For example, 70% of parents indicate they would enjoy donating classroom items and 58% would enjoy chaperoning field trips (WeAreTeachers & Volunteer Spot, 2013). Parent Heather P. recounts how one parent at her daughter's

> "Having children is like living in a frat house—nobody sleeps, everything's broken, and there's a lot of throwing up."
>
> — *Ray Romano*

school couldn't volunteer much yet got her employer to donate one year's supply of hand sanitizer and tissue to the school (Edutopia & GreatSchools, 2014). Offering choices to parents increases your chances of securing involvement.

Get the Whole School on Board

Your efforts to involve adults in your classroom will be easier if you can get the whole school on board for:

- **boosting community involvement.** Schools cannot achieve their goals until the community values education (Waldron, 2014). Encourage your administrators to implement proven ways to boost schoolwide community involvement. District administrators can coordinate with local libraries and organizations to reap districtwide wins, whereas school administrators can rally support from specific neighborhoods.

  For example, a school or district can hold a contest in which each city council member or each local business owner (both groups who value good publicity) can be challenged to bring in the most community representatives to a community member meeting at which needs are shared and people's involvement is penned down. Media can be present to promote the winners of this contest.

- **boosting parent involvement.** It's hard to ask people to volunteer when they are used to being unasked. This predicament is especially common at the secondary level. Rather, if parent and community involvement is a schoolwide movement, people are more likely to volunteer and to offer you more hours.

  Administrators should also be encouraged to implement ongoing recruitment and support efforts. At K–4 Technology Facilitator Kevin Jarrett's school, recurring training days are offered for volunteers and are met with a great turnout, and this provides a steady volunteer supply on which staff can rely (Edutopia & GreatSchools, 2014). Levine (1993) offers a myriad of timeless ideas, such as training bus drivers (who often see parents the most) as recruiters of parent volunteers, leveraging local business donations to reward parents for volunteer time, and promoting male and female parents of the month.

- **Recruit parent volunteers.** Parents and other family members are the obvious stakeholders from which to solicit involvement, but the approach must be effective. Parents report preferring teachers contact them online or through email regarding volunteering opportunities, yet 64% of teachers ask parents to volunteer through fliers and notes sent home (WeAreTeachers & Volunteer Spot, 2013). Facebook seems to be the primary social media tool parents use (Larkin, 2015), yet this can change over time. Preferences can also differ (e.g., online access is limited in some communities), and you might want to ask parents what they prefer to be sure you reach out to them appropriately. In his Free Technology for Teachers blog (www.freetech4teachers.com), Richard Byrne (2015) suggests Celly (http://cel.ly/), Feedblitz (http://feedblitz.com), Hootsuite (https://hootsuite.com), and Remind (www.remind.com) as free technological avenues for communicating your announcements to stakeholders. Using a combination of approaches can help increase your response rate. See the "Maximize Back-to-School Night and Open House" section of this chapter for more ways to recruit parent volunteers.

- **Involve parents in homework.** Yurij Halushka recommends assigning homework that requires family participation, such as cooking with a parent and writing the steps they took or interviewing a family member about a particular topic (Edutopia & GreatSchools, 2014). This provides the pair with quality time while increasing parental awareness and support of class endeavors. Be sure you have options in place for students with absentee parents, such as letting other mentors complete the assignment with the child if a parent is not available.

- **Recruit retirees as volunteers.** Question: What better volunteer could there be than one with years of teaching experience and plenty of time off to remain rejuvenated? Answer: None!

Working with Retirees

See the "Grading" chapter for guidance in how retirees' time might be spent and what support retirees might require.

Recruit the help of retired teachers who still want to contribute to their profession. You might start by asking retirees you know, but don't stop there if none will commit. You can ask principals within and outside of your district to connect with retirees who might be interested.

You can also post your need on online educator forums or request organizations or publications to get the word out (see those listed in the "Tedium" chapter and eResources for possibilities). Think of senior citizen organizations in your area and the teachers' associations of which you're a member, then give them all a call. If you nab a helpful volunteer, your search time will be a fraction of the help time you get in return.

> "Internships give you all the experience of a summer job without the hassle of a paycheck."
> — *Stephen Colbert*

- **Recruit the help of student teachers.** Aspiring teachers often possess energy, enthusiasm, and text-based knowledge. In addition, they are often searching for a classroom in which they can learn and meet their institution's requirements for hours spent student teaching.

Though you will likely devote time to mentoring the student teacher, the added help time (such as lesson plans he or she writes and teaches) typically supersedes your own. I know a teacher who student-taught an entire summer school class in which the paid teacher was never present (the student teacher literally never met her "mentor," who merely left her a box of textbooks). That arrangement clearly isn't recommended or ethical. Rather, it demonstrates that student teachers can prove to be fairly competent teachers. In the mentorless teacher's case, she completed the summer with no complaints, and her students progressed in class.

Speak with your administrators about your desire to work with a student teacher. You and your administrator can also reach out to school and district administrators within and outside of your school district, as well as local universities that offer teaching programs.

Working with Student Teachers

See the "Grading" chapter for guidance in how student teachers' time might be spent and what support these aspiring teachers might require.

I was shocked to learn my principal heard "no" from other teachers at our school before getting a "yes" from me to place a student teacher in my classroom. I couldn't imagine turning down the added help, but many teachers do. In other words, it can be easier than one would think to acquire a student teacher for one's classroom.

Communicating Across Language Barriers

Mary Cowhey, profiled in Nieto's (2015) book on teachers who last in the profession, collaborated with parents to start Familias con Poder (Families with Power), a group for parents and guardians who are not native English speakers and generally never graduated from high school but who now provide a morning math club helping 25 to 40 students per hour twice per week. When I was a teacher on special assignment at Buena Park Junior High, we employed the Parent Institute for Quality Education (PIQE; www.piqe.org) to reach out to parents in their native language, predominantly Spanish, to take part in an 8-week program that armed parents with the knowledge to support their children in school and be active volunteers. The graduation ceremonies for these parents—many with no more than a third-grade education—were crowded with family members as proud as if it had been a college graduation. These parents' involvement surged, and students had more effective advocates at home.

Encourage your administration to implement a program designed to target parents often missed by traditional communication efforts, and arm these parents to help at your school. Also, be sure all of your communication with parents and community members are translated into their native languages, and that non-English speakers are given ways to communicate with you in their home languages (e.g., the contact information of a district translator through whom they can schedule calls and meetings).

- **Recruit men.** Men are often not approached for involvement opportunities with the same frequency or expectations as women are. When few or no men in students' lives contribute to the classroom, it shortchanges the teacher and students, and it sends a poor message about gender roles. If you offer a variety of volunteer options (e.g., not all dads enjoy decorating the Valentine's Day banner . . . not that all women do either), make it clear to parents that you expect both genders to contribute equally, and reach out to dads with gusto, you can win over allies for the profession while increasing parental involvement.

- **Encourage your school to offer parent workshops.** Whereas parent–teacher conferences occur only a few times per year, parent workshops keep parents continually involved. For example, Federal Way Public Schools hosts workshops in which parents learn how to support children's academic achievement and advocate for them in the school system (DeNisco, 2016). PIQE, mentioned earlier, is another example of such a program.

- **Host a curriculum day or night.** A national survey involving 17,563 responses revealed parents (87%) participated in general school or parent–teacher organization meetings more than any other school activity (Noel, Stark, & Redford, 2015). Yet other school or classroom events can be equally compelling. Cooper and Sinanis (2016) suggest inviting parents and students to work on a learning project together at school or hosting a bingo night in which the game is interrupted by curriculum-related demonstrations. Such activities provide families with bonding experiences, improve school–home relations, and involve parents directly in learning processes.

College Costs Can Be Covered

Parents' support of academics can increase when they know sources like these can help pay for college:

- College Abacus (https://collegeabacus.org)
- Free Application for Federal Student Aid (FAFSA; https://fafsa.ed.gov)
- Raise.me (www.raise.me)
- Scholly (www.myscholly.com)

- **Focus on involvement that matters most.** Castro et al. (2015) reviewed 5,000 studies to find 37 notable studies involving more than 80,000 students and families. Parents' expectations, discussion of school activities, and support of reading habits had the greatest impact on children's academic achievement—far surpassing homework supervision and participation in school activities. For this reason, any efforts to cultivate parents' support in the first three ways are especially powerful.

Parents' Expectations

Of parents of students in grades 6 through 12, 36% of parents expect their child to earn a graduate degree, 28% to merely complete college, 17% to merely attend college, 9% to merely graduate high school, and 1% of parents do not expect their children to finish high school (Noel, Stark, & Redford, 2015).

Avoid Parent Pitfalls

Sometimes despite our best efforts, communication with parents turns sour. Taking proactive steps can ease the pain of confrontations and protect you if a parent retaliates against you.

The following strategies are effective examples of such steps. Apply these strategies as appropriate for your circumstances:

- **Keep diligent records of prompt communication.** Some district calling systems help you automatically keep records of phone calls, emails, and face-to-face conversations with parents. Even without such tools, maintaining a record of each correspondence is crucial and will save you future exasperation. Note the date, time, mode (e.g., phone number you called), and a note (e.g., left a message for Parent A about child throwing a pencil and asked for call back). These logs can prove helpful during parent conferences. Also, if problems escalate to meetings, possibly with administrators in attendance, these records will support your points, help you appear as the proactive professional you are, and will often prevent an unfair conversation (e.g., the parent claiming to not have been informed of his child's ongoing problems in your class). Respond promptly to any parent contact, even if it is to suggest a meeting for further discussion, and this diligence will assist you in the same way.

Hablar Mi Idioma

Twenty-five percent of students have a home language that is not English (Nieto, 2015). Fliers, calls, and other means of communication should go home in the languages parents speak. Most districts have translators who can help, and students and volunteers can translate in many cases.

- **Counter negative with positive.** When a parent seems against you, praise can often turn him or her around. Educator and difficult parent expert Allen Mendler (2013) recommends conveying your care for the student and your respect for the parent with something like, "I must tell you how lucky your child is to have a parent who cares as deeply as you do about her to be as angry at me as you are today . . ." (p. 1) and connecting on having high hopes for the child. This puts you on the same side and illustrates your devotion to working in the child's best interest.

  Ninety-six percent of students report their parents care about their education (QISA, 2014), and the parent's willingness to speak with you indicates he or she wants what is best for his or her child. Listening to the parent more than talking is also recommended.

- **Cut poor communication short.** If a conversation turns sour, such as if the parent raises his or her voice or insults you, you should not endure the hostility. Doing so is not only unhealthy for you, it is also a waste of time for all parties. High school history teacher David Cutler (2014) recommends ending offensive conversations with something like, "I hear you're upset, but I no longer feel comfortable speaking with you on the phone. We should meet face to face, but with an administrator also present" (p. 1), and then reporting to his department chair. Involving supervisors helps protect you against unjust accusations and improves the next conversation's chances for success. The scheduling of such a meeting also gives the parent cool-down time. Be sure to frontload such supervisors with your account of events and related evidence to ensure the meeting stays on track. Seventy-eight percent of parents agree that sometimes parents unfairly blame schools for issues that ought to be a parent's responsibility (NBC News Education Nation, 2015), so the parent could come around before the meeting. Yet be prepared regardless.

183

- **Outmaneuver time-zappers.** Some parents are kind yet all consuming. They contact you excessively or request an unreasonable amount of communication or effort from you. First, do your best to let the parent know you value his or her input and are working hard for his or her child. If these parents sense they are being blown off, they can become more clingy or transform into combative. Also, you want the student to benefit from the parent's passion.

  Second, introduce the parent to technology that will answer the parent's questions for you. For example:

  - Score on a test? Overall performance? Look at the online parent portal's student-specific data dashboard.

  - What assignments are coming up? How to best study for a test? Look at the class webpage.

  There are many free, powerful edtech tools you can use even if your school district doesn't provide any (see the "Technology" chapter). Not only do well-picked tech tools save you time, they empower stakeholders to answer their own questions when possible. If the parent struggles with the tools, get the parent in touch with the school district's IT department for help.

  Finally, explain to the parent that—while you're happy to answer major questions—it's important you're each focusing your time on efforts that *directly* help the child. If your time is spent on tomorrow's lesson plan rather than talking about it, you can better help the child. If the parent tutors the child rather than talking about the kid's need for added help, he or she can better help the child. You might need to repeat this explanation until the parent breaks a needy pattern.

- **Communicate with parents regularly.** A study (Kraft & Rogers, 2015) conducted through Harvard University and Brown University involved 435 high school students enrolled in a credit-recovery program and their parents. When parents were sent weekly, single-sentence messages on how their kids could improve academically, those students failing to earn course credit reduced by 41%, home discussions improved in quality, and the course dropout rate shrank by nearly half. Messages you send home do not have to be lengthy or time consuming to have an impact, which makes your job easier in the long run.

  If you are tech-savvy, www.mailchimp.com is easy to use and can allow you to send messages to all students' parents simultaneously while appearing to be contacting them individually. You can vary the messages and recycle messages when they apply again. The "Technology" chapter describes other tools that make communication easy.

- **Invite input.** Find opportunities to solicit parents' feedback. When parents feel you value their input, it strengthens your bond with them and suggests you welcome their involvement in your classroom.

  You can request parent feedback both informally and formally:

  - Informal example: when discussing Tess Tur's behavioral struggles, ask her parent, "What have you found to be effective when Tess throws a tantrum at home?"

  - Formal example: add a link to the parent portal for a survey on whether parents are having a hard time providing the materials for the at-home science projects (note the survey is anonymous).

- **Use a proactive email plan for regular communication.** Some teachers prefer communication via email, as it provides a clear record of communication, can be easily referenced, and can often be faster than phone conversations. Other teachers find typing responses consumes time and

> "Some cause happiness wherever they go; others, whenever they go."
>
> — *Oscar Wilde*

  find the phone to be faster. Cutler (2014) adds tone and meaning can often be misinterpreted via email, and this can compound emotion. Determine which approach to email use saves you more time and direct parent communications into your desired format. Plan to break from this approach when necessary (like when a hard-to-reach parent only responds to text messages or when you need parent involvement requests to reach parents in their desired forms of communication).

- **Resolve to maintain a positive mindset.** This can be hard, but it will aid you in the long run. Mendler (2013) recommends viewing parents as misguided advocates with something to teach you. He notes anger is better than absence, as this fury is fueled by a desire to help one's child, and that virtually all parents will work with you if they trust in your care for their child.

- **Share student accomplishments with parents.** Whether a student is always well behaved or the student's shining moment was a long time coming, it is worth telling parents about it. Yet in a survey of 66,314 students, only 52% of students said teachers let their parents know what the students did well (QISA, 2014). Though this takes added time, it helps keep you immersed in your successes, contributes to student success, and improves your odds of getting parent volunteers, all of which combat teacher burnout. This can be as easy as scribbling a quick note on paper (printed with your name) as students exit the classroom and handing it to the student to hand-deliver at home.

As sixth-grade English teacher Kechia Williams (2016) notes, something as simple as, "It is such a pleasure to have Brian in my classroom" (p. 2) can surprise and delight parents. Dr. Kimberley Palmiotto suggests sending a positive note home with one student per day with the request parents also write something positive about the student on the note's back side and return it to class (Edutopia & GreatSchools, 2014).

Actively Promote Good Publicity

While public perception can seem capricious, you can help outsiders see how spectacular you and your colleagues are. The following strategies can help you generate good publicity for teachers, and many ideas in the "Tedium" chapter can promote the profession and yourself. Apply these strategies as appropriate for your circumstances, which means skipping any that require time you don't have or skills you abhor putting to use (e.g., not all teachers love writing):

- **Dress for success.** It should go without saying that you should behave professionally (arrive early for Open House, have the room immaculate and handouts ready, etc.). However, teachers often underdress. Evidence from multiple studies confirms wearing a suit makes you feel powerful (Slepian, Ferber, Gold, & Rutchick, 2015) and that wearing high-status clothing causes people to cooperate with you more readily (Nelissen & Meijers, 2011).

- **Invite the media.** I worked with a fantastic science teacher named Dana Glidden. When she was doing a lesson on cell structure, she arranged for a local news station to come and film her. The students were required to face forward so their faces were not captured on film, due to our inability to film students without parental permission, but Dana's expertise was vividly captured for the evening news. Everyone watching got to see how skillful and valuable a teacher can be. Contact your local news stations and newspapers and invite them to one of your special lessons or events.

- **Make a production.** Parents and community members show up in droves for school plays, holiday sing-alongs, and other events they deem "official productions." Invite students' families and community members to class activities you present as crowd-worthy productions. For example, when students give class speeches, call it "Student Speech-athon," ask your principal and school board members to attend, and promote attendance as if it were a school talent show folks wouldn't dare miss. If you would find this taxing, of course, this recommendation is not for you.

- **Write, present, and produce public relations (PR) pieces.** Current teachers can contact TEACH (www.teach.org) to become a trained TEACH ambassador, which involves promoting the teaching profession. Meanwhile, the U.S. Department of Education invites teachers to join a national conversation about their profession in which teachers can inform future policy and programs. Teachers can get involved in the department's RESPECT Project (www.ed.gov/teaching/national-conversation) or expand opportunities for teacher leadership through the department's Teach to Lead Initiative (http://teachtolead.org).

The "Tedium" chapter covers other ways in which you can share your expertise with the world, such as by writing an article for an education magazine or presenting a workshop at a conference. These represent great opportunities to promote the profession as well. Keep your comments highly respectful of the profession, and provide a sense of how your topic fits in with the school's grander-scale endeavors to help kids.

- **Encourage administration to put out PR pieces.** School PR is crucial. When schools have bad images, higher-performing students end up at schools outside their neighborhoods regardless of zoning (saying they live at a friend's address, private school, school of choice allowances, or vouchers—concerned parents will find a way). This makes the school environment worse for all students and educators.

Ask your administrator to actively improve school image, such as by sharing school achievements with media or mentioning school efforts (e.g., the after-school STEM Club) in the School Accountability Report Card. As a teacher on special assignment, I made a school brochure (highlighting accomplishments) that our principal set in the school lobby and cleverly shared with local real estate offices.

Reflection Exercises

The following items can be answered individually and/or discussed as a group.

1. List five things you will do to make the most of Back-to-School Night and/or Open House.

   A. _____

   B. _____

C. _____
D. _____
E. _____

2. List five things you will do to make the most of parent–teacher conferences.

A. _____
B. _____
C. _____
D. _____
E. _____

3. Describe a well-rounded plan you will utilize to get many adults involved in your classroom. Be sure to appeal to varied adults with varied schedules.

_____
_____
_____
_____
_____
_____

4. Imagine you have a parent who becomes increasingly aggravated about your dealings with his or her child. What are some things you would do to improve the situation while preparing for the worst?

_____
_____
_____
_____

5. Imagine that same parent becomes combative on the phone and yells at you. What do you do?

_____
_____
_____
_____

6. What are some things you can do to reach out to the community, provide insight into great things you do in your classroom, and thus promote your profession?

_____

_____

_____

_____

References

Bantuveris, K. (2013, September 13). 5 tips for engaging parent volunteers in the classroom. *Edutopia*. Retrieved from http://www.edutopia.org/blog/strategies-for-engaging-parent-volunteers-karen-bantuveris

Byrne, R. (2015, June 18). How to get your school announcements to as many people as possible. *Free Technology for Teachers*. Retrieved from http://www.freetech4teachers.com/2015/06/how-to-get-your-school-announcements-to.html?utm_source=Edsurge Teachers&utm_campaign=af0dda9d1b-Instruct+182&utm_medium=email&utm_term=0_3d103d3ffb-af0dda9d1b-292335873#.VcOQ4JNViko

Castro, M., Expósito-Casas, E., López-Martín, E., Lizasoain, L., Navarro-Asencio, E., & Gaviria, J. L. (2015, February). Parental involvement on student academic achievement: A meta-analysis. *Educational Research Review, 14*, 33–46. doi: 10.1016/j.edurev.2015.01.002

Cooper, R., & Sinanis, T. (2016, January 13). Five ways to build your school's instructional brand and connect with families. *EdSurge*. Retrieved from https://www.edsurge.com/news/2016–01–13-five-ways-to-build-your-school-s-instructional-brand-and-connect-with-families

Cutler, D. (2014, March 21). 8 tips for reaching out to parents. *Edutopia*. Retrieved from http://www.edutopia.org/blog/tips-reaching-out-to-parents-david-cutler

DeNisco, A. (2016, February). Districts work to bolster parent involvement. *District Administration*. Retrieved from http://www.districtadministration.com/article/districts-work-bolster-parent-involvement

Edutopia, & GreatSchools. (2014, May 1). 19 proven tips for getting parents involved at school. *Edutopia*. Retrieved from http://www.edutopia.org/groups/classroom-management/783266

Harvard Family Research Project. (2010, October). *Parent–teacher conference tip sheets for principals, teachers, and parents*. Retrieved from http://www.hfrp.org/var/hfrp/storage/fckeditor/File/Parent-Teacher-ConferenceTipSheet-100610.pdf

Kraft, M. A., & Rogers, T. (2015, April 20). The underutilized potential of teacher-to-parent communication: Evidence from a field experiment. *Economics of Education Review, 47,* 49–63.

Krantz-Kent, R. (2008, March). Teachers' work patterns: When, where, and how much do U.S. teachers work? *Monthly Labor Review,* 52–59. Washington, DC: U.S. Department of Labor, Bureau of Labor Statistics.

Larkin, P. (2015, April). Say it with social media. *Educational Leadership, 72*(7), 66–69. Alexandria, VA: ASCD.

Levine, J. A. (1993). *Getting men involved: Strategies for early childhood programs.* New York, NY: Scholastic Inc.

Mendler, A. (2013, April 26). Rethinking difficult parents. *Edutopia.* Retrieved from http://www.edutopia.org/blog/rethinking-difficult-parents-allen-mendler

NBC News Education Nation. (2015). *Parent toolkit: State of parenting: A snapshot of today's families: A national survey of parents for NBC News.* Retrieved from http://www.parenttoolkit.com/files/ParentingPoll_PrintedReport.pdf

Nelissen, R. M. A., & Meijers, M. H. C. (2011, September). Social benefits of luxury brands as costly signals of wealth and status. *Evolution and Human Behavior, 32*(5), 343–355. doi: 10.1016/j.evolhumbehav.2010.12.002

Nieto, S. (2015, March). Still teaching in spite of it all. *Educational Leadership, 72*(6), 54–59. Alexandria, VA: ASCD.

Noel, A., Stark, P., & Redford, J. (2015). *Parent and family involvement in education, from the National Household Education Surveys Program of 2012.* NCES 2013–028.REV. National Center for Education Statistics, Institute of Education Sciences, U.S. Department of Education. Washington, DC. Retrieved from http://nces.ed.gov/pubsearch

Pappalardo, G. (2011). Engaging parents: An elementary teacher's field guide. *Edutopia.* Retrieved from http://www.edutopia.org/blog/parent-involvement-student-engagement-gaetan-pappalardo

Provenzano, N. (2014, October 8). Conference time: Chatting with parents. *Edutopia.* Retrieved http://www.edutopia.org/blog/conference-time-chatting-with-parents-nick-provenzano

Quaglia Institute for Student Aspirations. (2014). *My voice national student report 2014.* Retrieved from http://www.qisa.org/dmsView/My_Voice_2013–2014_National_Report_8_25

Reid, K. S. (2014, May 2). Survey: Most teachers want involved parents but don't have them. *Education Week.* Retrieved from http://blogs.edweek.org/edweek/parentsandthepublic/2014/05/survey_finds_most_teachers_want_parents_in_their_classrooms.html?cmp=ENL-EU-NEWS3

Riggs, L. (2013, October 18). Why do teachers quit? And why do they stay? *The Atlantic.* Retrieved from http://www.theatlantic.com/education/archive/2013/10/why-do-teachers-quit/280699/

Sledge, N. (2016). *Keeping high school parents involved & informed*. Retrieved from http://www.scholastic.com/teachers/article/keeping-high-school-parents-involved-informed

Slepian, M. L., Ferber, S. N., Gold, J. M., & Rutchick, A. M. (2015, August). The cognitive consequences of formal clothing. *Social Psychological and Personality Science, 6*(6), 661–668. doi: 10.1177/1948550615579462

University of Phoenix. (2015, May 4). *K–12 teachers rate the ability to affect students, lifelong learning opportunities and the variety that exists in the field as top reasons to join the profession, finds University of Phoenix survey*. Retrieved from http://www.phoenix.edu/news/releases/2015/05/top-reasons-to-join-the-education-profession.html

Waldron, J. (2014, June 12). A teacher's tough decision to leave the classroom. *News Leader*. Retrieved from http://www.newsleader.com/story/opinion/columnists/2014/06/07/teachers-tough-decision-leave-classroom/10170567

WeAreTeachers & Volunteer Spot. (2013). *Parent volunteers in the classroom*. Retrieved from http://www.volunteerspot.com/Parents-Volunteer-In-The-Classroom

Williams, K. (2016). *9 techniques for building solid parent-teacher relationships*. Retrieved from http://www.scholastic.com/teachers/article/9-techniques-building-solid-parent-teacher-relationships

Wilson, M. B. (2011). Tips for new teachers: Making the most of parent-teacher conferences. *ASCD Express, 6*(12), 1–2. Alexandra, VA: ASCD.

Conclusion

15 | Get Started and Keep Going

Think of the advice you give your students, even in the face of adversity. You probably say things like, "Don't give up. You can do this. Believe in yourself." Well, you need to believe what you tell your students, as the same is true of you.

Pounce on your biggest burnout-inducers knowing you are worth more than burnout can give you. Little steps add up to big steps. Start with strategies you can handle best, and move on to new strategies as you are able.

> "In the midst of winter, I found there was, within me, an invincible summer."
>
> — *Albert Camus*

You are a teacher. You are a hero and this world's greatest chance at progress.

You will not drown in the challenges around you, because the only one who knows best how to be a teacher *is* a teacher, and if you were brave enough to begin this calling, you are brave enough to follow it all the way. Enjoy the peace and success that awaits you there.